so Luminous *the* Wildflowers

AN ANTHOLOGY OF CALIFORNIA POETS

EDITED BY PAUL SUNTUP

TEBOT BACH • HUNTINGTON BEACH • CALIFORNIA • 2003

Editor: Paul Suntup
Assistant Editors: Mindy Nettifee, Michael Paul, Steve Ramirez
Introduction: Michael Paul

Design, layout, cover design: Melanie Matheson
Cover photography: Roland Harrison, John Kaiser
Printed by: Westcan Printing Group, Winnipeg, Canada

ISBN: 1-893670-13-9
Library of Congress Control Number: 2003101777

Tebot Bach, Welsh for *little teapot*, is A Nonprofit Public Benefit Corporation which sponsors workshops, forums, lectures, and publications. Tebot Bach books are distributed by Small Press Distribution, Armadillo, Ingram, and Bernhard De Boer.

www.tebotbach.org

This anthology was made possible by a grant from **The San Diego Foundation Steven R. and Lera B. Smith Fund** at the recommendation of Steve and Lera Smith.

Dedicated to the memory of Solly Suntup

(September 1, 1928 – May 9, 2002)

so Luminous the Wildflowers

AN ANTHOLOGY OF CALIFORNIA POETS

EDITED BY PAUL SUNTUP

CONTENTS

INTRODUCTION

When my family came to California, my father got the hare-brained and beautiful notion of prospecting for gold, a hundred years too late for the rush. And so he did it. With a wife and two children in tow, he accepted the offer of a mine owner in the Trinity Alps, just outside of Hayfork, to blast a drift into a mountain with fifteen miles of mine shafts already in it, and if he found a rich new vein, to go 50/50 with the owner. That man was a grizzled, old-timer named Kelly whose life had spanned from the nineteenth into the twentieth centuries. He had been an amateur prospector himself, until he found a promising outcrop of quartz on that mountain, and staked claims in his name and that of every relative he had. After seven years of work on a mineral claim, title to the land changes to the claimant's, so by the time we arrived there, Kelly owned the entire mountain, and had taken several fortunes worth of gold out of it.

We lived in, and my earliest memories are of, an anachronism. A kind of last outpost of the Wild West, with all the classic elements. A town made up of tents and wooden buildings. A one-room schoolhouse. Very little law. Men were killed in saloon brawls, with no arrests or prosecutions following. It was a haven for all manner and degree of desperadoes, from tax and alimony evaders to hardened killers, with all their stories taking place in a valley of breathtaking, pristine beauty. And up on Kelly's mountain my father chased his dream, drilling and blasting his way into that mountain, until he realized that in doing so, he had probably brought his family into harm's way, and finally, quietly, folded his tent and moved south and into a more conventional lifestyle. I still remember the smell of dynamite, and the mountain, jutting up like an island from a white sea of morning clouds.

Gold. California. The two are so synonymous that there are one and a half million references to them on the Internet. Gold. It is all played out in *them thar hills*, but it is the reason I happen to live in California. We came for the gold and found it in the weather, the water, and the culture. My dad finally made his living in the shipyards of Long Beach, the third busiest port in the world, the city I grew up in. *Incidental Buildings & Accidental Beauty*, the first anthology from Tebot Bach, was mined, if you will, from the talents of Orange County and Long Beach, California. The editors believed there was something simpatico in the styles and sensibilities of Orange County and Long Beach writers to warrant bringing them together in the first anthology to do so. This time around we have enlarged our claim to include writers from all over this fabled state. And we have done some serious prospecting on behalf of our readers. Blasting our way through a mountain of submissions and following the promising quartz of first lines, we found pure literary nuggets that compelled us to preserve and present them here for your pleasure. We bring together in this volume 187 poets, including some of California's newer, promising poets as well as those who are established and widely published.

There was neither a unifying theme nor limits as to style, length, and content when the call for submissions went out. We merely wished to showcase, in all their varietal splendor, some of the poetic riches of California. It is 100% Californian. And it is 24 karat gold.

—*Michael Paul*

John Gardiner

Californian

At mother's funeral, a first cousin said to me,
"We're the older generation now, the story tellers,"
and I thought of my travels with mother
up and down the coast from Eureka
to San Diego, camping in lower Death Valley
or high in the Minarets, the boring grind up the 5,
childhood dreams in Grass Valley, Nevada City,
passing Mt. Shasta, strange mountain from the moon...

Our stops at Conway Summit, highest point on 395
between Canada and Mexico; sometimes we'd sing
to while the time and she'd tell me which tribes lived where,
the history of mining, stories of the Cornishmen,
and all the names of trees and flowers—when her father
traveled by horseback across the state,
he hardly saw his feet for two full days,
so thick and high were wildflowers, in fact
he never got the pollen off his boots and pants,
or so the story goes.

Driving south, headed for the great basin of L.A.,
thinking of five generations of Californians
that I carry in my blood, stunned by the endless
proliferation of cars, panoply of metallic colors
brighter than the sun, my old slow truck
plodding like a plowhorse, nothing but autos where
the wildflowers were, and I don't even know their names.

Poems

David Alpaugh

What My Father Loved About Melmac

That you could drop it on the floor.
That you could hit it with a sledgehammer.
That you could back over it with a Mack truck.

That in this Henry-J world where we rattled along
crying for a Tucker—here at last was *the real thing*.
That it came in a variety of colors including maroon.

That you could get it with S&H green stamps.
That once all 32 pieces were stacked up on the pantry
shelf you'd never have to buy dinnerware again.

That at last he could enjoy his Kix or Shredded Wheat
in peace—knowing every bowl on the kitchen table
was childproof.

That never again would Mom shout, "Butterfingers!"
nor grieve over china lying in ruins at our feet;
nor swear as she cut her toe on an unswept shard.

Pharaoh of our New Jersey duplex, Dad dreamed
of burial, near the Nile, with his favorite cup & saucer.
"Melmac," he said, "would last ten thousand years."

Hope Alvarado

> ...for a person who boasted of wooing
> death, she had proved the worst of
> teases—an elderly flirt of the sort
> she would have savaged in a paragraph.
> —Brendan Gill

Introduction to the Portable Dorothy Parker

Her teeth—
when she had them, were not enough
to keep her quiet.

Bloodshot in the morning mirror.
Late gin. Too many cigarettes.
Bound breasts. Tight pointy shoes. Her talent—
for ending things badly.

Makeup doesn't cover
the purple splotches
on an old woman's throat.

Pinched toes
and the taste of blood
loose the tongue—
snake it twice 'round her neck

tight enough to break capillaries
in the white of her eyes.

She didn't follow her own advice.

SJC

pebbles set in the walk trap water
black flickers dodge flannel
and denim, Nikes, boots and wheeled carts—
for a sip

little birds,
this is such a dreary place
to drink

a creek runs
Guadalupe side of the airport
there, only the stray sun will not see
the verdant flame captured
in your wings

Joy Arbor

Sometimes in the Car

I miss the conversations, the questions
you would've asked, the answers I'd give
to make you laugh but leave
you unsatisfied. I'd explain that the world
isn't fair, that the past only seems
better because it's over and known,
that an oak tree is just an acorn
a squirrel forgot.

If I had loved
you, the thought of you, more
than me, right now
you would be asking me why
the rain is falling
without relief.

Sometimes in the car, I wonder
if your questions would be the same
as mine. How big I would look to you,
full of answers and magical kisses.

I am not breaking to pieces,
an arm on the dash, a kneecap
in the glovebox, I am pulled together
gritting my teeth against judgment
against glib bumper stickers
against my own lips.
No loss, a vacuum
so slight, the pressure
of air against skin
stops hurting.

Carlye Archibeque

Things to say at a party when you don't want to be there.

I love these little mushroom thingies.

I slept with the host after he was married.

I like long walks on the beach at night.

I've always found low IQ's very attractive.

When I was five the baby sitter made me massage his penis.

I can only stay a minute.

White wine gives me a headache.

I've never killed a man.

Do you come here often?

I slept with the hostess before she was married.

I fully support our police department.

I wish foot binding would come back in style.

Have you heard the one about the dead poet?

I have herpes but it's not that bad.

I have a headache but it's not that bad.

I wish they'd bring out more of those little mushroom thingies.

I really have to be going.

Charles Ardinger

Island Music

A brain can spiral out like a galaxy
expanding away from itself
in one more excess of astronomical metaphor
the management regrets. The table
is only big enough anyway for one
spiral notebook, one's two or three drinks, and

the distance measured in light years.
Now figure out the next cleverest paraphrase
and make note. Future generations will sneeze
with awe to know the revelation coded in one's
odd program: no
one speaks the language here, and stars

fly apart because they were born
that way, and I'm one of them. A brain
can form a spiral as a hiding place and use
a cosmic simile regretfully to keep its distance, and we call that
space. It's notoriously cold and silent.
It's everyone.

Sylvia Bar

The Grail
(UCLA Years)

And we, who have waited,
Walking the streets by night,
Seeking the Grail...
Are the voices, outside our window,
Wanderers of the dry land.

And we wait, by the window,
Between the bell and the door,
And the stone wall around us,
Between I dare and dare not.

And the Grail, is a bird flitting by
Saying, "I'm just passing through."
And we still wait, by the wall and the window
For the end of a date on the wall,
A date beyond decision,
Cursing our second chance.

And the dry land, outside our window, dies,
Nervous and clipped like a blind crab.
And the voices, holding the key,
Between the bell and the door,
Like the wind, a lost way,
Plunge into the dry earth.

And we wait by the window
For the bird that passed through.
But all we see is the dry land.
Formal,
With a column,
And a blown rose.
Withered,
At its foot.
Tall.
Terrible.
Alone.

Dorothy Barresi

Love Koan
>   *for Phil*

Are you my prime meridian,
my arrow, my mend,
my paranoiac in all the right places,

my hardbound book
I won't put down?

My best, least sin?

Through all my numbskull wanderings
with lambs and pills and a quitter's luck,

how did I find this chill that sends
sugar to my bones?

Magnum mysterium—
my husband, my room.

In all the worlds this world soon builds
by real estate and rasp and awl
for bitter gods
eating deranged food,

how did you find in me
what I could not find
myself forever,

my birdsong avalanche?
My croon.

Terry Bat-Sonja

I Wash You

I wash your forehead,
then the hollow of your cheeks
like a mother cat.
The white soft cloth
gently covers you in sections
in the small hospital room.

On the bed, you sit with empty stomach
and pain, avoiding my mother cat ways.

I wash you warm.
I wash you clear.
I wash you new.

You sit like an angry absent Yogi,
cross-legged,

shyly, sadly, distantly,
you endure me.

Richard Beban

Summer Rain Sonnet
for the Average Housefly

"The housefly (Musca domestica) can complete its life cycle in
as little as seven to ten days."
—Newspaper Filler Item

When it rains, thick gobbets that plunk
on the sill with cadence of childhood
jump rope rhymes, even flies stay home.
And where is that, exactly? Small fecal castles?
A welcoming calf's carcass, smooth ribs brown
& regular as a bone marimba,
enough leather clinging to struts
for a makeshift umbrella? No. Let's say
home is the heaped white sweetness
of a giant sugar bowl, each crystal a cubist
delight a thousand times sweeter
in compound eyes—each short *Musca domestica* life,
though confined a day by rainfall, not brutish
at all, but tasty & worth a song of its own.

Marjorie Becker

His Jesus Feet

Before I knew him,
I looked for you, Paul,
walked railroad tracks,
picked flowers,
usually irises, stream lilies,
anemones, all reminders
of bouquets you once
brought.

That afternoon I'd told him
my truest favorites,
purple and lilac,
the shock of pinks
against my skin.
His Persian eyes,
moist when happy,
narrowed. He said,
"I don't want to know
these things. Too much
past. Too much
flesh."

I thought about leaving,
but that night we walked.
He stopped at fenced-in daffodils,
a yellow twilight blaze,
shed his shoes,
climbed,
pulled some flowers,
climbed back.
He found me,
worked the stems
into my long black hair.

I still thought of you,
still wondered what more we would be,
but just that night,
the golden catch upon me,
I walked him home,
took him in,
washed
his feet.

Michelle Ben-Hur

Tell Me Everything You Know About Mirrors
For Amélie, Carlye and Jennifer

Never look directly into one.
Rolls of flesh spill over the top
of your waistband and your face
puffs out like a fish. Your eyes are always red
and crooked; your tongue and lips are stained
from last night's fourth glass of wine
or fruit punch. Dresses you selected with care
and grace don't fit. Their colors are off:
white becomes oatmeal; yellow
is now olive; purple, puce. Your skin
dyes itself to match—green, chalky. Really,
I like to pretend it's a skyscraper
on a street in Tokyo, neon garish

at its head. I stride, determined
to be timely for my luncheon
with the fellow American I met
over too much saké the night before.
I wear my favorite blue jeans, black tank top,
no make-up except bright red lipstick. Jaunty,
I forget myself until I stop mid-step,
startled by a familiar and attractive woman
walking out of the building's reflection,
walking confidently into me.
I approach it slowly,
sidle up like a deer hunter,
my eyes careful,

squinted, until they see a pin-up:
slim, full-breasted, blonde, with eyes so blue
the sky blushes when they blink.
Nothing looks bad on her, so I spin
and smile and flirt with her image
until I make the mistake
of looking it in the eye
and the fantasy is gone,
replaced by a stolid, stony face:
gray skin, taloned hands, tumbleweed hair.
And I freeze, trapped
by the monster I've known since childhood,
the one who's funny, talented, smart.

Ayanna Bennett

The Shop

My lungs have missed this air
heavy with gospel and ammonia
like escaped southerners miss
the damp swaddle of August heat.

The walls fade around the edges
of dull sketches, styles a decade
out of date.
The brown paper
meant to hide its age only
draws the dark stains of old
rainstorms down from the ceiling.
Old women watch
their pocket books and grandbabies
through the bitter wheeze
of overworked dryers.
Girls in rollers hold copies of Ebony
to their almostbreasts,

And I am eleven again. Come
to hang my legs from the tall chair
and repent, at last, my bad hair.
The bigsmiling woman who fought
my nappy roots like unruly children
and wrung them straight in her
redbone hands is gone now.
Here her light skinned sister
stands ready to redouble the fight.
She has the heat of righteousness
in her aging grip.

Only she and Christ Jesus know
what it takes to make me right.

Even now,
with all else passed,
time and distance take nothing
from this, my black girls burden.

They only lengthen the drive back
to this place where I was first
dragged into womanhood
by my hair.

Dinah Berland

Water

Once Mars had an ocean.
Now it has only dust and ice.
Once you were a dowser, pointing
to places where water sublimes.
Now I am wandering in the desert,
obsessed by a mirage. Yesterday
an asteroid as long as a football field
nearly crashed into the earth. No one
saw it coming. No one knows
what saved us. There is no light
that does not come from darkness.
I am wandering in the desert.
The distance from earth to sun
is the yardstick for the universe.
I take a shower. Water trickles down
my back. I make coffee, feed the dog.
I am wandering in the desert.
This causes me to make
irrational assumptions; for example,
if only we could talk again,
then I would be happy.
I put on my red high-heeled sandals,
check myself out in the full-length mirror.
The curvature of space depends on
material and dark energy.
You had a lot of dark energy.
It was tricky backing up that spacecraft
to the asteroid Eros. The mockingbird
outside my teacher's window
is imitating Indian ragas, auditioning
for the Nature Channel. A small candle burns
in the center of the table. On a narrow
slip of paper, I write *mayim*, the Hebrew
word for water. Did you know that *mayim*
is the root of *shamayim*, the word
for heaven or sky? There is no light
that does not come from darkness.
I am wandering in the desert. This poem
is a prayer for salvation. This poem
is an answer to that prayer.

Mel Bernstein

Ragman

Somewhere, between
the four corners
of the universe
where four monks
sit and play
a game of marbles
there is a ragman
with his horse and wagon
asking for rags
to fill his wagon.

I can see him.

My mother, who is
screaming at my father
for not being able
to bring home
any money
cannot see him.

My father
who is being
screamed at
cannot see him.

My Russian grandmother
who lives with us
and tells me
Russian-Jewish stories
like the one
about Samuel
from the bible
whose face is stamped
on the backside
of the moon
like the imprint
on a copper penny
can see him.

My brother
who is four years
younger than I am
can see him.

And this ragman
and his horse
and his wagon
are made of stars
and the wheels
of his wagon
always moving
always moving
are made
from strings
of memory and light.

Seven Monkeys

They say
in an infinite universe
seven monkeys
given an
infinite amount
of time
can perfectly
type
the complete
works
of Shakespeare.

This begins
to happen
but
the last
monkey
screws up
the last letter
of
the last
word
and
you are
that monkey.

Wendy Bishop

Grass: A Museum

Everywhere it has a special name:
pampas, veldt, sedge, steppe.
We ask it to be boats. We ask it
to be watertight, to weave baskets;
blackbirds circling the lid,
to be masks, oriental breast plates,
mats and mule straps. We ask it
to feed, to build, to welcome bowling
balls, to spring under lawn parties,
to ignore the dripping teacups, to give.

Men travel thousands of miles
to get more. Animals kneel to it.
Cities fight it with whips and edgers,
pushmower, powermower; farms fight it
with scythe and combine. Children
get lost in it and roll backwards.
Men paint their porches green.
They worry when it isn't there
and threaten when it is. A woman
brought rattlesnake grass to America
to grow in graveyards and alleyways.
In Africa eat lemon grass and be poor.
In Los Angeles have a rock garden and be bored.
Talk about grass at every party.

This valley, the Sacramento, is full
of lush farms, of tomatoes, of tule
grass bordering irrigation ditches,
rattling anciently. Grass wins
the interiors of railroad tracks
and the flooring of abandoned houses.
On the low, fringing hills that entice
no one, grass flares through July, green,
burning into a slow, autumnal yellow,
serving no one, holding nothing.

Laurel Ann Bogen

Mystery Spot with Gaze Turned Inward

What vortex pulsates above my bed?
Sprawled among the flannel sheets
and four felines waiting to be fed,
he ponders these questions of ultimate
torque and consequence.
How the little wheels of his mechanism spin.
Great is his dynamo—a nuclear reactor
whirrs in his toothy Kenmore guarantee.

I stick to him like gravity—
an inescapable pull
impels my Volkswagen
down the 2 to the 134
hurtling past freeway exits,
taco stands and mini-marts
from Highland Park to Lake Street
past the tinted windows of Roscoe's House
of Chicken and Waffles,
the Planned Parenthood clinic whose clients
cup furtive joints in the parking lot,
the Craftsman house with the blue Christmas lights
where Lil' Kim blares from the porch.
Down the street, maple leaves pile
like dunes in his marvelous yard.
There, in the melting light, I stop
to measure the turbulence,
plant herbs, calibrate our inverse polarity,
wind socks flapping in the sun, an oscillation
of simple mysteries caught then funneled outward.

Derrick Brown

Pussycat Interstellar Naked Hotrod Mofo Ladybug Lustblaster!

How silly I get.
How lost and silly I get
unraveling my fingers
to where your arms connect.

I come to your body as a tourist.
Endless rolls of black and *wine* film in my fingertips.
Documenting the places that change your breathing
when touched with the patience of glaciers retreating drip by drip.
It reverses your breath back into the places
that trigger subtle curls in your purple painted toes

The breaths are not just worth 100's of sparrows,
but all the gray air sparrows die and wander in.

There are things about you I collect and sell to no one.
I journal them in a book you gave me with the inscription
"Don't leave your ribcage in the icicle air. Something will break."

I wrote about the courage my hand would need
aiming down the worn comfort of your hair,
hang gliding across the summer slits of your winter dress
searching the perfection in your rock and roll breasts,
stealing the heat off the drug of your stomach.

Let me die a white fang death
trembling on the snow and linen of your shoulder blades.

I want to buy you a black car
in 66 shades of black
to match the wandering walls of your heart
filled with the mysteries of space and murder.

Let me spend my days on the shores of Abalone Cove
collecting bottles that wash ashore and burning the messages inside
to fill them with new messages like,
"Send more coconuts."
"Send more coconuts and wild boar repellant."
"Wow, I'm on an island, please send my 5 favorite albums.
I've already built a victrola out of sand and eel doodoo."

I will float the armada of messages towards the Atlantic
and wonder if a pale girl in N.Y. spends time at the shore.

I will wonder if she can see the stars I carved our initials into
when I got all sick and weightless.

Lay in Bryant Park and look hard,
your last initial isn't up there
for it is worthless to me
since I had dreamed of changing it.

This is the love of mercenaries.
I'd kill an army of sleeping Cubans for the rum desires
in the clutch of your tongue.

Touché to your lips.
Touché to your way.
Touché to your ass.

You are an electric chair disguised as a La-Z-Boy.

My clear bones take shape in the mouth of glassblowers with asthma
for there is no perfection in me
but maybe clarity.

Crush me with the satisfaction of your black misted, un-clocked breath.
I always come back to the secrets and wonder of breath.
Yours is something for sparrows to wander in.

It's not that I wait for you;
it's that
my arms are doors I cannot close.

Mark C. Bruce

The Pompeiian Couple

Two men are carrying a mattress
in the emergency lane of the 5 freeway.
The pale yellow light of a car's
flashing blinkers catching them
in a bas relief, faces upturned
arms around the bulky mattress
like Greek warriors embedded
on a vase, black and red orange,
their arms stiffly raised,
Agamemnon and Odysseus
bringing a consolation prize
to Achilles, hoping its sagging pleasures
will sate his brooding need
to be attended to as if he were a god.

The woman in my passenger seat
has fallen asleep, her small lips
not curved in smile, her chin
low on her chest. It was our first date
and all of the walking through the gallery
of artifacts from Pompeii has worn her out.

I bought her a portrait
of a Pompeiian couple which had touched her,
a woman and her husband, holding pen and book
and gazing directly at the viewer
from two thousand years.
It had been found, a fresco
on the wall of a home buried
in volcanic ash. They seemed so content,
so sedate, that thin sense of longing
in their eyes not for a life they didn't have
but for the moment they could stop posing
and turn again to each other.

The woman beside me sleeps
and dreams, no doubt, of a villa
in a Neopolitan port suburb,
children's voices echoing against
the walls painted with gardens
and stiffly posed birds.

Somewhere in her dream is a husband
who doesn't look like me.

I pass the men carrying the mattress
and take the woman back to her home,
knowing there are some burdens
whose ends I will never understand.

Christopher Buckley

March 21, & Spring Begins
on Benito Juarez's Birthday in Mexico

In Mexico today, Benito, you are 193
springs beyond the sun—and in the village
of Ixtlan, there are no Zapotecs
left to remember.
              You are on my calendar
here in California, and this morning
there is the tablecloth with the crumbs
of despair left over from every democratic thing. . . .

Thank goodness the mockingbirds are starting up,
I had almost forgotten what world
I was living in—
              I turn from my desk to their dither,
their desires and grievances boiling up
with a new regime of light,
                  and I can almost
see the first golden stream of monarchs lifting
from the conifers of Michoacan,
                    their hearts
no heavier than mist releasing to the sun
as they guide back north through the industrial clouds,
past the loggers in complicity with the standard
corporations of death.
              Once, Benito, the trees pointed
the way and the stars fluttered above us like
Platonic ideals—
              I too gave assent to them
and everything larger than ourselves, but for days
I've been looking over the shoulder of dust—
which is everything that became of land reform—
and at times like these,
              the council of the wind
proves useless.
         If I have a soul, it's lost
inside my shirt—I always expected more
of my blood,
           which still sings of the sea,
the chorus of salt—but like the monarchs,
we are not even the dust we leave behind.

I deliver my petitions to the waves
and receive the recapitulation of loss,

which is the old response—the shells,
the seaweed, washing in with their worth.
There is no remedy in the maps of the sky;
the civic documents pile up against the poor.

I can propose anything on this bright new air,
but I won't hold my breath,
given the spindrift, the equivocations of light.
I no longer have a child's heart—
despite sea water in every cell,
the crystals of desire, the corollary
of the stars—their threads evaporating
for centuries on the surface
and representing nothing.
                              I resign
my failed scholarship, my love
of the stars. I make my interpretations
of the lemon and eucalyptus leaves—
I hide whatever belongings I have left
from the sky.
                President, old governor,
compadre in dust, all the theories fail—
it's only this ordinary bird who is bothered
finally, who still carries forward our demands.
From several possibilities each morning
we will reach for hope, every time, on the branch
of hopeless things.
                    Today, in our bare feet,
this new season is everything that's sure
on earth, the earth that will never be divided
equally among any of us—
                                at best,
and at long last, we drift through the air
no more than the dreams from trees.

Joy Buckley

Panties in the Trash

once in an alley
on the rich side of
Santa Monica near
the Blue Bus stop at
Harvard & Colorado
i found 6 brand new
Hanes for Her
Double X Large Ladies
drawers exactly my size
spilling from a plastic bag
store tags dangled from
the elastic waistbands
the cotton crotches were
soft and snowy white
what a mystery
who would toss
her clean underwear
next to a grimy trash bin
maybe a successful
weight watcher i thought
now a size 8 and no longer
in need of so much cotton
she is prancing around in
her Victoria's Secret thongs
while i stand undecided
beside a battered dumpster

Susan Buis

8 Little Stories about Hands

1.
You were almost born on a bus,
so your mother named you "almost flying."
Your hands turn to wings and brush the skin of your cheek.
Your hands turn to wings and scratch the air.
Your hands turn to wings and you're away.

2.
St. Francis blesses the birds in Giotto's Arena Chapel.
His blue-haloed hands form benediction
over birds transparent with age.

3.
Her vermilion stained fingers
break a rose into a fall of petals.
One hundred bracelets sing on her arm.

4.
I want to slap your face so hard
that you can see my fingertips on your cheek.
Instead, I wrap my hand around this rock—
it's smooth and iron-red, the size of my fist.

5.
"You were born to be the mother of two sons," she said.
I hold them, two tiny lines on the side of my palm.

6.
His hands were like a woman's hands,
delicate, tapered fingers, like pencils drawing circles
on the inside of my knee.
Calligraphers hands on a bulky laird's body.

7.
After the accident she prayed that if some part of him were paralyzed
may it not be his hands.
They were.
"I can still close them enough to wrap around a beer," he laughed.

8.
I treasure my hands; they hold the weight of your hair.
I love my hands; they verify that you are made of milk.
I cherish my hands; the light that reads you in the dark.

Stephen Burdette

Verlaine to Rimbaud

I did love him,

Pale filigree of eyes
                    and hair,
Brows that were gathered vales
                              above long eyelashes,
                              streamers of ebony satin.

In wine,
        I came to him,
    a gargoyle in love,
Vomiting the splashing water
                        of spilled drinks,
Espousing cultural formalities
                        of wooden stakes through the heart,
Spurting boulevards of blood
                        until I mummified him
                in bloody gauze.

Together, we ran with thin horses
                              which fed on rocks
                        and coal
                        and on the air,
Listened to cynical whoring oracles
                              who preached against all logical thought.

We traveled a highway of stamped down undergrowth
And like lunar fictions
                    of madness
                and green cheese,
        I promised to climb waterfalls
But realized only comedic operas
                              of Sodoms
                        and Gomorrahs,
Until I discovered
                waterfalls can only be climbed when frozen.
            and that there is nothing
        more innocent than

Virgin lust.

Mary Cahill

Vacation, One July

when I was just a child
we took a train to Denver

      tiny porthole of track and gravel
my sister Kate and I could see
every time we flushed the toilet

      awake all night

watching cows at sleep
      the first time I ever had
my own bunk
      the first time I ever saw

countryside fly by my window
in the dark deep of night
      farms and prairies
silos, lakes, and streams

      and then at last the mountains

shadow giants
white-capped and majestic

      and soon we would be on them

horseback on a trail
that would take us to the top

      the day I rode a chestnut horse named Amber
the saddle smelled of sweat

      and then she broke away

dashing down the mountainside
      holding on for dear life

      heart stopping
      hooves stomping

half terrified—half free

      the day my ear tore on a tree
      the day I beat them to the ranch
      the day a Navajo named Jake

took the feather from his Stetson
and handed it to me

    because he said I rode like the wind

Don "Kingfisher" Campbell

Story of San Diego

My wife, mi suegra and I sit
On the deck of an afternoon tour

Of the landmark harbor where white
Men first missioned indigenous lives

On this western half of the continent
Once unlabeled the four directions

We are shown the famous vessels
That fired on twentieth century possible invaders

A proud face beams about
The sparkling pacific water

You cannot even tell fathoms below lie
Detritus of five billion planetary revolutions

As distant skyline holds memories
Of wilderness in pastel-colored rooms

My family steps off the boat
To breathe the rest of our days limited

With small events chambered in temporary brains
That wait to join historical others in layered meaning

John D. Casey

*Minkowski**

everything is moving apart, they say, and usually i believe it.
they have proved many things with pen and paper
about bodies and triangles and cause.

there was a bent man at a desk
who realized that time and distance
are both just arrows pointing.
i see him watching a sunset with his wife.
"the sun is ninety-three million miles away," he might say,
"or eight minutes into the past."
she might say, "i love you," and the words don't reach him for a second.

* Hermann Minkowski (1864-1909); German mathematical physicist who combined space and
  time as elements of a four-dimensional approach describing relativistic phenomena.

Anniversary

you never had to wonder about such things as a kid.
after the requisite amount of flirting to assure yourself of a soft landing
and asking your friends what they thought
and asking your friends to ask her friends what they thought,
you would sit in her row at plausible denial distance
rip a corner from your math homework (or whatever class you liked least)
write any short paragraph in shaky handwriting containing the question 'will you go
out with me?'
trust in the unwritten code of left hand to right hand
and follow your question to its answer with your eyes.
maybe she would blush silently and give you a look that said 'ask me later.'
maybe she would write back something with the word 'yes' in colored ink and lots of
hearts.
or maybe someone in that chain would break the secrecy
leaving you to judge how much of her red face was thrill and how much was
embarrassment.

you asked me when i thought we started.
i didn't know.
we talked about it and you decided that it was sometime in november and for all i
know it might be.
it has never been easy since those paper days to tell when you step over that line
from one set of inadequate words to another
(and what's the opposite of 'serious' anyway?)
you might think it happens when you have to hunt for your bottle of shampoo
among the three or
four which are suddenly in your shower
or find strands of her hair in rooms which used to hold other memories.
you might think it happens the first time you can be naked with her in sunday
morning daylight
with your tangled hair and stubble without using her eyes as a mirror.
you might think it happens the first time she trips on a staircase in front of you and
you wrestle with gravity for just a moment, as if you had a chance to win.
you might think it happens when you start writing poems about other women with
the names removed
because you never have time for them in any other way.
but watching you drive away through an unexpected twilight rain
i start to think it happens the way the raindrops paint the ground:
slowly and then all at once.

Mary-Marcia Casoly

Proof on the Verge, 1905

I knew before hooves
hit the dirt, this morning Papa
would be bringing round
our new delivery horse and wagon.
Mama Rossini and Mrs. Persoglio
were downstairs, elbow-deep in flour,
a dash of salt, silver scoop
still in the sugar sack;
the sky buttermilk white.

Scent of fresh loaves
tempted me, my chores waiting.
But I stayed,
unnoticed at the window,
nightgown sleeve grazing the curtain.

Uncle Stephano held out his camera,
framing the picture. Our bread
for the first time would be going beyond
this Oakland neighborhood.
Papa held the reins, always looking so serious,
his eyes nearly covered by a dark brim,
but his bushy mustache,
parted and combed, betrays
his excitement.

The hand-painted letters
on the side of the cab were beautiful:
French American Bakery
not: French Italian baking
as it says above our store.
Once I asked, which one of us was French,
and Mama Rossini said none of us,
but our customers expected sourdough.
They want Parisian.

Susanna Casteel

Espiritu

You came to me, finer than morning,
an unguarded form in gauze.
An arbor breeze tickled the night,
touched me, guileless and pure.
I wrapped myself in you.

The lift enticed me to feel my way
through a shadowed lane, racing heart tamed
by darkest green and black, ignorant faith
in search of something feeling like childhood.
A flame rose inexplicably as I drew closer
to a fusion of heat and harmony.

I've been a vagrant on roads that tempt
with promise—insignificant, unanswered nights.
Days have been dusky without your artistry,
sun hiding behind clouds.

In this oasis we are as we were before—
praising the pines and the mulberries,
still giving thanks for sparrows.

An outcast branch illuminates two huddled finches,
befriending pale hands that shape them
in papier-mâché. Like small rosebuds,
they turn their creamy petals
with unearthly motion
to create their own light.

Carlota Caulfield

Serial Fugue for a Deep Breath*
(So Unforgettable, Nashville)

Before he died, Tai Zang asked
To be buried with the scrolls painted
By his favorite artist. My hand jerks and
Makes a crease in the paper so the
Ink will flow.
Savoring the mint tea
And Toshie's Scottish anemones
On wing, arch and river, with the Roman
Bridge at Pietra, while
Being a tourist sitting on its border.
Inhaling what it is granted you to live
Quick arrival at the other side of the border
Without knowing what you've gotten to live until
You draw near with unheard of speed
While the stones roll down the slope
And the radio station transmits
A program to calm its listeners
And the fullsome voice of the announcer
Urges drivers to stay off the highway.

I remember the word mistletoe.

I've come to Nashville equipped
With a wheeled suitcase, a biography of Houdini,
And an essay about the Sephardic Jews of Mallorca that
I'll read a few hours from now.
My face furrowed, a face that also reflects the
Precise and precious savor of fatigue. Dark marker of the newly arrived
Trying to echo her, I hum along with Reba McEntire "What if it's you,"
As the shuttle passes through a city that means nothing to me.

I let a cowboy cab driver lead me to Music Road
What does it matter, I've got all the time in the world
An infinite thread of saliva runs with perverse slowness into the pillow
And immediately I go back to being more of a foreigner
Than the 42-foot high statue of Minerva
In the Nashville of my childhood fantasies.

The mind's domain is pure invention, memory's scar ever there
Any story would be too long to tell, and anyway
I don't remember the names of my idols when I was six.
There's a distance of hundreds of broken records
And of melodies I can no longer hum.

A crossing defined in a glance of blind inks,
Invisible cuts on skin and the memory of the memory itself.
Memory and hand entwined with memory and hand,
and a tongue that sculpts and establishes and becomes fixed
through pure habit of air: its mouth.

But celebrating and blessing my childhood doesn't cost me anything
Provided that the letter to the Three Kings doesn't turn into
An obsession, or my cowboy boots into fashionable rags.
The biographic note would be of no use whatsoever if my mind weren't
Bursting with the ceaseless accompaniment of a continuous bass fiddle
And my head weren't rocking in a cinematographic rhythm of delicate
And complex brush strokes. More memorable than any personal confession
Is the enchanting and playful circus photograph where I'm the little girl
Held in suspense in a "Havana Western."
Nashville makes me dream like mad,
And has even stirred up my double's enthusiasm for endlessly finding fault
I should accept that before and after my trip, there has been lots of water
under the bridge.
Let's leave it at this so we don't have to talk about tone-deaf people, frayed
passions, and entire worlds falling apart.

I climb the steps to my hotel in my boots sticky with muddy rain,
A persistent memory of some scratch on
A window. I could even feel it like a pale recollection.

* Title of a musical composition by
María Teresa Prieto (Oviedo 1896-México 1982).

For Genaro and Janet Pérez.

Translated by Mary G. Berg and the Author.

*Fuga serial para aliento**
(So Unforgettable, Nashville)

Tai Zang pide antes de morir
que lo entierren con los rollos pintados
de su artista favorito. Salta mi mano y
abre una zanja en el papel para que
corra la tinta.
Delicia del té de menta
y de las anémonas escocesas de Toshie
en el ala, arco y adige, con puente
romano de la Pietra, mientras se
es turista sentado al borde.
Respiración de lo que te tocó vivir.
Rapidez del otro lado de la frontera
sin saber lo que te tocó vivir hasta,
aproximarte con rapidez inaudita,
mientras las piedras ruedan cuesta abajo
y la estación del radio lanza al aire un
programa para calmar a la población,
y el locutor en pastosa voz,
ruega a los automovilistas
que se mantengan lejos de la carretera.

Recuerdo la palabra muérdago.

He llegado a Nashville equipada
con una maleta de ruedas, una biografía de Houdini,
y un ensayo sobre los sefarditas de Mallorca que
leeré dentro de varias horas.
Grietas en mi cara, así como cara que da el sabor preciso
y precioso del cansancio. Oscuro signo el de la recién llegada.
Con tentativa de eco tarareo con Reba McEntire "What if it's you",
y afuera del shuttle una ciudad que no significa nada para mí.

Me dejo guiar por un taxista-cowboy hasta la Music Road.
Qué más da, si tengo demasiado tiempo.
Un infinito hilo de saliva cae con perversa lentitud sobre la almohada,
y de inmediato vuelvo a ser más extranjera
que la estatua de Minerva con sus 42 pies de altura
en el Nashville de mis fantasías infantiles.

El suelo de la mente es puro gesto, y la cicatriz sigue en su lugar.
Cualquier historia sería demasiado larga de contar, y además
no recuerdo los nombres de mis ídolos a los 6 años.
Hay una distancia de cientos de discos rotos
y de melodías que no logro tararear.

Travesía que se define en una mirada de tintas ciegas,
cortaduras invisibles de la piel y el recuerdo del recuerdo mismo.
Memoria y mano abrazadas con memoria y mano,
y una lengua que esculpe y establece y se fija
por puro hábito de aire: su boca.

Pero celebrar y bendecir mi niñez no me cuesta nada,
siempre y cuando la carta a los Reyes Magos no se me convierta
en una obsesión, ni mis botas de vaquero en harapos del gusto.
La cita biográfica no tendría utilidad alguna si no fuera porque
mi cerebro bulle con el acompañamiento incesante de un bajo continuo
y mi cabeza posee un ritmo cinematográfico de brochazos
delicados y complejos. Más memorable que cualquier confesión personal,
es mi fotografía circense, ensoñadora y juguetona en la que soy la niña
en suspense de un "Western habanero".
Nashville me provoca un onirismo de todos los demonios,
y hasta ha desencadenado el entusiasmo de mi doble, siempre colando faltas.
Debo aceptar que antes y después de mi viaje, ha habido mucha tela para cortar.
Quedémonos aquí para no tener que hablar de personas de mal oído,
pasiones mal hilvanadas y mundos enteros en trozos.

Subo las escaleras de mi hotel con mis botas de lluvia pegajosa,
una memoria persistente de cualquier arañazo en
una ventana. Incluso podría sentirlo como un pálido recuerdo.

*Título de una composición musical de María Teresa Prieto (Oviedo 1896-México 1982).

Para Genaro y Janet Pérez.

Michael Cirelli

Lucky Penny (for Catholics)

Look at you,
laid out on your back,
self worth next to nothing
and helpless.

I've swallowed blood and chipped teeth
that leave less sour a taste in my slack mouth—
the most honest slave master
since Franklin I suppose.

Still, somehow I pick you up.
Somewhere, in a gray whirlpool
at the bottom of the wishing wells of my eyes
copper synapses fire in my brain
and I rescue you like a lame puppy.

Amongst loitering lint
and shiny quarters for laundry,
you jangle like a good idea,
a notion I'd like to hang onto.

I can translate you into a squirrel nut,
a stale piece of gum.

I can attribute you to a royal flush
or my first breath in the morning,
say, how lucky I am to be alive—

It seems like the older I get
the more pennies I collect,
Saint Christopher's charm trembles on my chest,
a compulsive crucifix hung above my bed.

I wonder when shall I emancipate you
to a cranky cash register,
how long to cradle you in my pocket
before your luster depreciates?

I busy myself
blowing out candles,
crossing fingers and whispering Hail Mary's
from the bottom of my sacred heart.

Jeanette Clough

Learning to Swim

My mother is terrified of water. She'll stand
in the shallows, dip nose, chin, cheeks
and come up squinch-faced, fighting droplets
that threaten to drown her. She hatches
a fish-child. Arms pressed into my body,

I steer with sidelong flashes; hold my breath
long as possible in the opaque quarry
pond, playing aquatic hide-and-seek
with her worried shoreline gaze.
She signs me up for swimming lessons

when I am five to separate us both
from her fear. The pool is clear,
unnatural. Black ribbons stretch across
a monochrome floor. The instructors
wear whistles around their necks, tin shards

jabbing the sun. I learn to take in air
at the third stroke's pull, to exhale
bubbles. One day they let us out early.
Nobody is there to pick me up so I decide
to walk. When my mother arrives

the children are gone. Fright rising,
she checks the bottom of the pool then drives
back and forth on all possible roads
to find me treading steadily,
shedding scales, thirsty for home.

Marcia Cohee

Minotaur

i

Life is surreal
and we've all seen too much,
keeping up those little fictions
no matter what the weather is.

The gods have abandoned us to this.
All the years we've counted and judged,
measured our bodies against time, hoping
for some inventive trick of language to fill
this long void, this imagination.

Into the quiet torture, another night,
dim and dreamless, moon gone,
tea lukewarm, truth sleeping
as far through breakfast
as the light allows.

Habit lifts us out of February
toward intermittent sun
and the stray amusements of a Sunday afternoon,
lyrical and subdued in brilliant ironies of the soul.
Here we linger, waiting for something we cannot name.

ii

Windows altogether red
and chairs
that pool blood at your knees.
A cold rain, obsidian streets.

Who sleeps? Who helps you
find the thread? An older woman
dreams alone: this is my body.
The inaction, the empty bullring.
We know our place.

Knives are hollow, spoons are blunt
and I have nothing to say.

I know the forecast
but I cannot discern the weather

your arms make.
I don't mind the rain.

iii

Sometimes you listen to your own dim voice
as it carries across the room.
The light is bad, and you are
easily ignored. What will never be.

His claim is not immortal, but he is, he is.
And the stars are there to no avail,
no guiding us through the maze.

This is the time of year to buy underwear
and sleep through the crooked days
of spring. There is no nunnery, no cloister,
there is no place of mere devotion
where we, like tonsured monks, will go,
adding a few more lines to the poem,
waiting for the dark age to pass.

In the belly of glaciers, the moraine, the rock's hollow,
the loess that's blown and blown until it covers the sea.
In the end of what's fertile and summer's demise.
In the way we carve civilized time from pagan ice.

Earth on its spindle
wandering ellipse of constellations,
white bull in a labyrinth, white cow in the meadow
which one is made of wood?

Hear the minotaur, the passions that create him.
This will end the way it ends, defying our translation,
neither ice nor fire.

iv

His hooves tucked neatly
under the tablecloth: this is the part
you cannot see.

I know he must be a god
if you are this queen
like Pasiphae facing Minos down:
now, you have taken my dreams.

While Daedalus and science are conjuring
where to put the thing.

And we, who sleep by day
and work by night, know
these limits. Any garment
may be worn. Like
suicide's human presence,
beyond the wisdom of beasts.

The bull is white and she is white.
Who can explain absence of moonlight?
Black thread of moonpath
on the sea where Pasiphae
turns her wooden silhouette:
this is my body, the patient moon,
the almost tangible air.

I peer into the well of centuries
and know the darkness,
which is my name.

Larry Colker

Referent Madness

If it's to be pot luck
I can bring *frengira*—
the dance of dolphins before the bow.

When it comes time to bulldoze
all the pitted, exhausted words
into a mass grave
and bring out the new,

I will be ready with what I have saved for years:
venublastiphor:
one who is incited to murder by beauty,

and *boolk:*
the sound a bowling ball makes when dropped
into an active volcano.

Some words we probably can never do without:
anencephaly, blur.

I vote we keep *massage*
but change its meaning
to *emerald breeze.*

Let new words flood over us,
rebaptize our snarling tongues,
but let us be cautious,
avoid mistakes of the past,
accept no word ending in *ism*—
for that way lies madness.

Cathy Colman

Night Swim, 1974

It's the amnesia of the future,
all the green rooms of summer sealed up.

That's how I saw it then, a failure to be enough,
like a cup of spit you must drink to please

your host. The first time I met him at the party
he said, "You know they're pretty sure the mind

isn't located in the brain" and the nightpool
we swam in rippled in the windless

air. The ranchhouse filled with famous
poets and dead poets seemed to be at the party

too, with hair the color of sand, their thought-ghosts
flickering in the eucalyptus leaves. While he explained

relativity to me in layperson's terms, pods split
by the pain of carrying their seeds

fell and floated on the water. I pointed out
the *treeness* of the tree, as the frontier

of the party pushed forward onto the patio. The turquoise
pool lights gave him a horror-movie glow, but he

looked so beautiful returning from his own
death, his throat pulsing the way mud does

during rain. I wanted to be his skin's
intricate servant.

The party came to a stalemate,
as they tired of suddenly dull pleasures.

The older male poets had spoken enough
wisdom, the younger gathered around them and

the very drunk had dropped to their knees, possessed
and holy, suffused by that moment

when angels come out of things. And somewhere cherries
ripened in their basket, and the later-to-be famous female

poet's lemon hair signaled like a beacon over all of us.

How To

The secret is to rise early.
Listen to liturgical collisions in the jazz riffs.
See how that square of sunlight foreshadows

a bigger radiance in the day.
Drink strong tea. Get up and sing
a lively song. Or re-enact Galileo's discovery

of a heliocentric universe. Sorry, I meant
Copernicus. Then peel hard-boiled
eggs that roll wildly around the plate

reminding you vaguely of dating.
Slice the eggs so you're surprised
by the gold coin yolk and how painterly

they look on the blue Fiestaware
next to the Early Girl tomato. Now
you might begin to suspect that

some duty needs to be discharged—phone calls
made, bills paid, or perhaps a fresh
elucidation of Oliver Wendell Holmes' aphorism

"We will twist the tail of the cosmos 'til it squeaks."
But resists these mandates. Just laugh,
like Republicans at welfare.

Sit down at your desk. Whack the piñata of childhood
until something ugly flies out. If you can't
find a subject, stare out the window.

Wait for an image to announce itself, or the mail-
person, whichever comes first. Or use
a phrase from another writer's poem to get going.

For example: "The secret is to rise early."

Alison Cotter

Remote Control

Have you ever wished you could fast-forward the sun?
Mute your mother-in-law?
Pause the stock market?
Have you ever wished

you could play some morning in reverse
so when you walked into the office and hit
the answering machine, you only heard
"tnedicca elbirret a neeb s'ereht"?

Then your finger lifts from the machine
and the briefcase that had fallen to the floor
leaps into your hand. You back out the door,
down the hall, across the street and all the way

to your parked car, which backs itself home.
There, the smell of coffee evaporates
as the machine sucks the drips up. Your suit
attaches itself to a hanger, the hanger to a closet.

The alarm switches off and you fall
onto the pillow and push the covers back
over your head as the bright of morning
reverts to the blue of dawn, the black of night—

the night the van speeds through the red light
into the intersection, straight for the car
that carries the friend who, at that moment, is alive.

Royal L. Craig

A Former Sweetheart

Then there's the kids,
Their noise and sweaty bodies,
The wet shoes, the dirty socks,
And always something strange
In their pockets.
My husband with beer cans,
Cigarette butts, and magazines,
Finding ever fresh corners
Of the house to decorate.
My mother-in-law
Knowing better than me,
Sooner than me
About every detail
Of every happening
In my life.
My brother who told me so,
And then telling me
That he had told me so.
The thirteen in-laws,
Turkey-vulture-like,
Whispering in hulking groups,
Waiting for my marriage
To stop kicking and die.
The gang at our parties
Poor-thinging me to pieces
For the bruise under my eye,
And the other stuff.
I keep busy
Ignoring everything.

Ruth Daigon

A Whiff of Chaos

in a caesura between now and then
we cling to the time
when looking back was sweet
a dream of open space
of nights fragrant with feathers
and a carapace of stars
instead
we have snapshots soaked in vinegar and honey
the failed revolution and days gone to scrub
the car's lost in longterm parking
our pockets flapping inside out
there's dust to water down
sheets to air
and the mirror no longer casts its spell
but
so far the sky's still there
sunlight climbs from the latest dark
as the new day hovers like surprise
and before we lie in the stone throat of sleep
we breathe the scent of buds nippling from branches
of ripe mornings random as vines
or listen to the terse comments of rain,
the hovering business of hummingbirds
and marvel at the luster of lightning bugs
or the crystal stretch of spit hanging from a cat's yawn

it's the best that we can do
not much
unless
it's everything

Carol V. Davis

Garden

I check the squash growing outside
my small screened window.
This morning the lip of a leaf has curled
in longing towards its neighbor.
We can chart this growth,
half an inch a week, unlike my babies,
who wake one morning into childhood,
and just as suddenly, demand I walk
two steps behind them.
I think of my friend, diagnosed with leukemia,
three children, pregnant with a fourth.
Illness has transformed her.
Her skin the grey-green of eucalyptus bark.
If I could transport her to my garden,
surround her with new growth—
The Satsuma plum with its promising flowers,
the rampage of healthy ficus.
Her shoes would dissolve in the peat-laced moss.
Her feet would grow roots.

Lucille Lang Day

The Gambler's Daughter

Before I knew my ABCs I learned to deal.
I performed at Daddy's Friday night
poker parties. I got to stay up late,
a good thing: I was afraid of the dark.
Sometimes, alone in my room, I saw the nights
as a deck of cards, stacked against me.

On Sundays Daddy and I fed the ducks
at Lake Merritt. Mallards scrambled for crumbs.
Swans drifted past the caged bald eagle.
Canada geese everywhere. Their calls
mingled with the bells from Our Lady of Lourdes,
and coots swam in pools of orange light.

I learned to read the handicaps when I was six.
I picked Lover's Dream and Lucky Lucy,
and Daddy took my bets downtown to the bookie
with his and Mama's. Mama and I sat
on her bed, beside the radio, fingers crossed.
She gave me fifty cents whenever she won.

At Steinhart Aquarium Daddy and I saw
batfish, flat, shaped like fans with yellow
tails and fins. Their eyes, black-banded,
twitched while they swam, mouths small pink slits,
opening and closing as they came toward me,
my hand in Daddy's, my nose pressed to the glass.

I looked into their eyes, liking them
better than the rockfish or eels, better
even than Ulysses, the bug-eyed bass.
They seemed to have a message for me
that I couldn't decode. I watched, wondering
if they knew what I knew: they were trapped.

I got my first jackpot when I was seven,
at the Cal-Neva Club just before breakfast.
Daddy shooed me back to the table. I could
hardly swallow my pancakes. He came back
with a red plastic cup filled with nickels
and a stack of keno tickets for me to mark.

I pretended I was the only daughter
of the Brownings or Curies, though there were no
books of poetry or science in our house.
Mama read *TV Guide, Modern Screen*
and *True Confessions*; Daddy read *Playboy*,
murder mysteries and science fiction.

I was never very popular with the kids
at school, though I taught them how to play
spit in the ocean, California poker,
lowball and five-card stud. I kept an extra ace
up my sleeve, but I rarely used it. I learned
to take chances; I knew how to bluff.

Lea C. Deschenes

West Coast Elegy

My love,

I lament that this calm ocean does not feed us,
that the palm trees do not shower us in green,
that the oranges never blossom,
and the sun only burns.

I have prolonged this Persephone summer
as long as I could, eaten
seeds behind my hand,
counted the pennies
laid on the eyes of the dead,
not enough.

When we wed, you knew it
to be a hawk and raven marriage,
bound to migration by the pull of earth,
of shapes forever shifting,
seasonal departures,
temporary perches
on an unending journey.

Winter overtakes us
in a flurry of fir and wintergreen,
the air, sharper, thinner by the minute.
In the cold, best to be in snow,
the feathered insulation of it.
Desert winter is a sharp bite
and no blankets.

To warm us,
there is only the pyre of our furniture;
all our nest and buried treasure, burning;
the ash remaining, hung in the breeze;
the mark of us, lasting
long into December.

Let the Samhain night be merry,
music and laughter attendant,
let us not forget what we love
in the losing.

Join hands,
rejoice in flight
and the one thing
the underworld
will never take.

Diane Dorman

Carpool Karma

It wasn't the jade green Jaguar
or the cobalt blue Corvette
that roused me from my carpool coma,
but the faded-beige Volkswagen bus
humming along like a happy sewing machine.
The driver, dark bearded,
long hair in a ponytail.
I was heading south, he north
when we made eye contact
across six lanes of traffic.

He smiles and suddenly it's 1967.
I'm floating in a canyon somewhere,
sunset peaking over the rim,
air cool and damp,
sage wet against my legs
as I walk the narrow path to the cottage.
The screen door moans softly
swirls the pungent cloud of incense
and flickers the candles hanging in macrame.
In the bedroom, mattress on the floor,
Indian-print bedspread draped from the ceiling,
sitar playing madly from another dimension
and there beneath sun rays
filtered through stained glass,
he meditates, eyes closed, his black hair
falling in waves over his shoulders
Ommmmmmm ommmmmmmmm
Mmmmmmmmmm Mmmmmmmmmm.

Deborah Edler Brown

Faultlines

> The fault, Dear Brutus, is not in our stars,
> But in ourselves...
> > —*William Shakespeare*.

She looks unshakable.
Under the lush tangle of red and gold,
behind clear azure pools, moon whispering mouth,
soft floral lawn, you know she is steady
as rock. Beauty so effortless
you want to set your clocks by it.

You forget that below the surface
the lines are already drawn,
fractured blueprints for sudden **violence**.

Before the rise of soft hills
and the scoop of hollow curves,
before time and weather carved cheekbones into her face,
something split in her formation, leaving gaps
to protect what she can't remember.

She is a fragile ecosystem. Her foundation
trembles when the tremors start,
toppling all constructs, all pretense
that she can escape her nature.
Tension builds when there is no motion.
Tension demands release.

Earthquakes are not betrayals
of strength, but of expectation.

Faults are in our stars
and in ourselves.

Ellen

The Idea of an Infinite Number of Stars
                            —Christopher Buckley

At nine I walked sidewalk squares
        under a canopy of maples,
        the space between leaves so small,
        light shone through like stars.
        Improbable in a city called Newark.
        Leaves turned the most angel-lipped red
        in autumn, when all there was to do
        was gather the fallen, like a street-sweeper,
        and sink in.
At nine I never knew
        I could have picked up a small rock
        and concealed it in my hand
        on the night I was followed
        down the walk
        by a ghostly man.
        Those young, colorless boys knew
        on that dark-moon night of ghosts
        in Dylan's Wales.
At nine, if fish were served,
        Mother hovered over me
        to catch needle-thin bones
        before they threaded themselves
        into my throat.
        My dead mother trails me.
        I don't believe in insubstantial souls,
        but such pure devotion
        has made a meat-lover of me.
Let me be clear.
        The boy who told me he'd take care of me
        when I get old, has forsaken me. No matter.
        I had laughed
        and vowed I'd never be taken care of.
        Said I'd swim toward Catalina
        on a new-moon night when stars hide.
        In that black, cold water,
        I imagine there is much that will matter.

Maria Ercilla

Wicked Weather

It is wicked weather outside.
The heat moves past us in waves
it is so thick
and even our saguaro cactus
has sweat beads on its blood-red blossom,
and your leg draped over mine
sticks to my flesh
then slips off
much like dreams
and love do
once the fever breaks.

John Olivares Espinoza

Why I Decided to Stay in School

I'm writing a poem
In the dim light of my living
Room, when Albert, the youngest
Of my brothers, walks in
Complaining about his job
At the Metro 8 Cinema,
And tells me about
Sweeping the floors,
Pushing through the tidal surge
Of popcorn, Milk Duds, Good 'N' Plenty,
And the remaining few soggy tortilla chips
Left over from a large nacho
A customer spilled along with his Pepsi.
He tells me about
The difficulty of cleaning
The kernel popper every night
And how the chlorinated smell of semen
From a high school blow job
During the matinee makes him
Want to puke, and how he leaves it
For Carlos Padilla to clean
On the next shift.
He tells me of his eight hour day
At four-ninety an hour,
And the demanding voice
From his menthol-breath supervisor,
Echoing in his ear.
And he tells me how
On his break, Juan Ortiz,
The Junior class bully,
Called him out to a fist fight
'Cause they don't get along in class.
He shows me the lump on his
Eyebrow caused by the stealth blow,
But tells me how he proudly finished
The asshole with four of his weakest jabs.
He tells me how he missed dinner
'Cause of work
And how they tried to feed
Them a microwaved ham,
And how he was glad he refused
To eat it because it made

Everyone sick in the gut.
He looks in the fridge,
Complains about there being nothing
To eat but cheese and vanilla pudding.
So we drive off at 10 p.m.
In his '89 Beretta for a late dinner,
But nothing is open in Indio,
No McDonald's, Del Taco, or Burger King.
He swears at the desert night
As his stomach growls like one
Of its coyotes,
And I tell him nothing is open
Because it's Thanksgiving night.
"I forgot," spills out from his lips,
And we disappear
Away from the crime lights like ghosts.

Carrie Etter

Sunday Afternoon

Who neglects the wind at its groaning
        stands in the warm, semi-sweet
chocolate and butter scent of a kitchen.
        Nostalgia's not the right word
for this loitersome disarray, nails spattered
        with batter and flour on
the blouse. My aunt, I never knew her to
        bake cookies, and if I'd had
a brother, he'd have liked the walnuts my
        sisters hated. There is sun
on the grass, I can see it from here,
        felt it on my back or the oven's heat
I attributed to the sun and turned to
        the window and the wind and
licked a finger clean. I would not call it
        longing, the shirt hung from
a branch and flapping; I would not
        name it at all.

Lawrence Ferlinghetti

History of the Airplane

And the Wright brothers said they thought they had invented
something that could make peace on earth
(if the wrong brothers didn't get hold of it)
when their wonderful flying machine took off at Kitty Hawk
into the kingdom of birds but the parliament of birds was freaked out
by this man-made bird and fled to heaven

And then the famous Spirit of Saint Louis took off eastward and
flew across the Big Pond with Lindy at the controls in his leather
helmet and goggles hoping to sight the doves of peace but he did not
Even though he circled Versailles

And then the famous Flying Clipper took off in the opposite
direction and flew across the terrific Pacific but the pacific doves
were frighted by this strange amphibious bird and hid in the orient sky

And then the famous Flying Fortress took off bristling with guns
and testosterone to make the world safe for peace and capitalism
but the birds of peace were nowhere to be found before or after Hiroshima

And so then clever men built bigger and faster flying machines and
these great man-made birds with jet plumage flew higher than any
real birds and seemed about to fly into the sun and melt their wings
and like Icarus crash to earth

And the Wright brothers were long forgotten in the high-flying
bombers that now began to visit their blessings on various Third
Worlds all the while claiming they were searching for doves of
peace

And they kept flying and flying until they flew right into the 21st
century and then one fine day a Third World struck back and
stormed the great planes and flew them straight into the beating
heart of Skyscraper America where there were no aviaries and no
parliaments of doves and in a blinding flash America became a part
of the scorched earth of the world

And a wind of ashes blows across the land
And for one long moment in eternity
There is chaos and despair

And buried loves and voices
Cries and whispers
Fill the air
Everywhere

Jack Foley

After Seeing the Film, Malena

Dearest Senora Malena,

You understand that it is particularly difficult for me to write this e-mail since I am
not only a child but a fictional one—one appearing in a film. But, after all, you are
a fictional character too, though not a child. To tell you the truth, I have been
watching you for years. This is no strange thing, since everyone in this town watches
you all the time. But I am the one who stole your black panties. I hope it did not
inconvenience you too greatly. Such beautiful things must be scarce in wartime,
especially when one's country is *losing* the war. Your great beauty inspires me daily.
Most of the men who see you want to go to bed with you. I am no exception to this
rule. When my father brought me to a brothel, I chose a whore who looked like you.
(I do not mean to imply that the whore resembled you in any other way.) However,
I think that my feelings are not limited to the sexual. You may have heard, when I
briefly went mad, I recited poetry. I think I must believe in the soul. Perhaps I con-
fuse you with my soul. For a child, the world of adults—and, for me, the world of
war—is like a movie I watch, just as I watch you. I see it going on and I am even
touched by it, but I can't influence it. It ignores me. I hope you will forgive me for
saying that your life, though undoubtedly real to you, was a kind of movie to me. I
can't express to you the pain I felt when I saw you beaten by those horrible women.
Yet what could I do? Only watch. Had you seen me—which you did not—you would
have seen me grow or struggle to grow out of my childhood. I got my first pair of
long pants. My father brought me to a whore, who was the first woman ever to make
love to me. The significance of such moments was not as great as I hoped it would
be. Twice, though, it was permitted to me to touch you, in a small way. Once, I
wrote a note to your husband. (I wrote many notes and poems to you but could not
deliver them.) And once I helped you pick up some oranges you had dropped. These
were, for me, my first real passage into adulthood, not my long pants or my first
sexual experience: these were the moments when I realized I could do something,
however small, to help another person. This, oddly enough, was my entrance into
manhood. It was also the moment when I stepped out of the movie—or, more
accurately perhaps, into it. I wish I could return your black panties to you.
Unfortunately, my father discovered them adorning my forehead and my mother
subsequently burned them in disgust. I hope you will not think it crude of me to say
that I know another who sometimes wears black panties. You were my first love.
You were also the first person I could truly help. How memorable that makes you.
Perhaps your beauty has faded, though I doubt it. Perhaps you have begun to forget
the events that happened to you in our town. It was not a bad town, though some
very bad things happened in it. For me, it was the place in which love, finding some
very unlikely tinder, burst into flame.

Yours Sincerely,

Renato Amoroso

Michael C. Ford

If Marriage Is Just A Bad Joke,
Take My Wife...Please!

> Lou Costello: A husband is what's left of a
> sweetheart after the nerve has been killed.
> —*One Night in The Tropics* 1940

if you were my wife, I'd buy you
rocket fuel for all my moon landings
on the bridge of your nose,

I'd negotiate with hurricanes
for your hairspray,

I'd steal Milwaukee blind by
washing your eyes in beery waterfalls,

I'd take prairie schooners to the shores
of your flowery Kansas mouth,

I'd play courts of sensual Wimbledons
to bounce between your slams, your advantages,

I'd be an indirect object in hysterical
conjugations of your accusative cases;

if you were my wife, you would icepick my heart
in the cold storage room of how I love you

Randall Forsyth

Eleven-Thirty P.M.

There is,
and then there is not.

A fine weave
of mercury and ice,
the storm clouds
drifting.

Saturn rising.

This is my heart.
Study, say nothing.

A long time ago,
there were people
walking where
you and I walk
and they said
and did differently
than us.

They got old as
we too will get old.

They fell toward
Saturn.

A fine work of study.
A weave of silk and
dye stuffs.

Pillows. Breathing.
Shelter from
rain and sleet
that burns everything
it touches.

I say this.
You do not.

I begin to drift off.

FrancEyE

Waste Basket

Kathleen
asked me
to keep it for her
when she moved out with the rest of her stuff
about two years before she died.
It's purple, enameled metal, in an open mesh, a
section of a cone maybe a foot and a half at the base.
About a year later she asked me if I still had it.
I did and still do, but I didn't tell her where.

Some time along in there I had more garbage saved up
to take to the compost heap
than I had time or strength to carry,
so I put it all in a white plastic bucket I had
and left it out on the balcony
to wait for me to feel stronger.

When flies mushroomed
I remembered her purple mesh wastebasket,
inverted it over the bucket, shooing them off,
and forgot about it…
It's been sitting that way ever since.
I suppose I thought it would magically disappear.

It didn't disappear but through the rains and sunshine
it turned into odorless compost,
a sweet reminder of Kathleen and the days
we used to make Swedish Bitters
on the same balcony, using
vodka I think and the herbal paste
she got somewhere in the valley.
It was great for healing little bumps on the skin,
but it couldn't help Kathleen with her genes
nor me with mine. She's gone and I'm here but failing
and I can't get the wastebasket off of the bucket
nor can I carry the bucket any more
if I could.

Today in the mail, Poets and Writers
asked me to tell them how I think they could help me
with my career.
I'm a poet, but what I need
is not an editor but some strong person

to come get Kathleen's wastebasket
off of the bucket for me
and carry the heavy compost
down to the garden
before my landlord
comes around to inspect.

This wouldn't affect my career,
Poets and Writers,

but it would be nice.
Thank you for your offer of help.

Amélie Frank

A Fourth Page Towards Immortality
        for Peter Sharp

No one can blame you for being pissed off.
Even Dr. Kübler-Ross, in her stroke-hampered state
is livid as the Dickens at her lot in life, what's left of it.
She hates that she is hobbled, rails at her spirit guides
for keeping her exquisite mind alive while her body
winds down in fits and starts. The first death is always
the most inelegant.

The second death, true, is the sadder one, to be
extinguished so completely when the cells that carried
someone's memory of your rake's smile,
the musicality of your voice, the tenderness
of your hands as you threaded surgical steel
into the veins of the fallen wink out one by one,
oblivion gathering speed as entire organ systems shut
down. When those who loved you move on, they
take with them the remembered joys of the inner eye and ear.
Even your helixed legacy, carried in the hum and spit
of your currency and their currency's currency may not
be mindful of your restless spirit swimming in humorous spirals
at the level of mitochondrion and the carnival of inevitable mutation.

As consolation, I can offer you this fourth page, the first one
that is not salted with my longing for you, the first one anchored
in the permanence of what you will always mean to others,
dinging joyously at the level of platelets, weaving radiance into
the fiber of every sheet of paper that speaks of you.

Currency is an Australian slang term for offspring.

You Awake?

There is in my narrow bed
a pillow as long as my body
against which I align myself
as I lie on my side, imagining us
as two of Moore's fallen bronzes
our hips sweetly proximate
my totemic belly warming
your eunuch's back
my left nipple ever introspective
the right, a beacon of ripeness
alert to the shift in the climate
or that joke whispered only
in latitudes cozy with
the Tropic of Capricorn.

Richard Garcia

Furry Louis Drops in on Surrealism 101

Right now, your eleven year old girlfriend
is laughing in your ear while you're galloping,
down Waller street with her on your back,
and you are eleven years old too, now you're
thirty-five holding Julian in your arms,
he weighs ten pounds, and has been here
for one day if you don't count in utero
or eternity and you say, The moose is loose
and you can feel your shirt splitting open
at the chest while you're shooting
through swinging dislocates on the rings,
lucky it is summer and even your sweat
is mixed with the smell of fresh cut grass
lucky your sixteen year old girlfriend
is watching and you are sixteen too, now
you see a note pinned to a door
while on your way to a night class
Furry Lewis visits Surrealism 101 tonight
so you enter a dark room and Furry
limps in rather sprightly for someone
who thinks he might be ninety and
has a wooden leg, followed by a worn-out
young man from the blues festival
assigned to pick him up at the airport
two days four nightclubs six restaurants
and three parties ago and Furry plays a slow,
bluesy, slide-guitar rendition never
ever recorded of Bicycle Built for Two
and he whoops and throws his guitar
in the air and it spins three times around
before he catches it and Furry laughs to see
the currents of Katherine's hair streaming
across the pillow as if someone could copper-leaf
the wind and Van Morrison is going crazy
on a love song spitting out Meet me
at the pylons, you can meet me at the pylons,
meet me, and right now at the pylons
a bonefish picks up the fly you tie, shoots
out the length of your line and your buddy,
who you thought came to a bad end
under house arrest in Mali, smiles at you
so I won't ask what time it is now because

you're busy and anyway now will be gone
before you can answer, which is odd,
because now always seems to last forever.

Amy Gerstler

Buddha Sonnet I

Awake among sleepers, he knows
the hypnotist's loneliness. Robed in clusters
of bubbles, skull cup in his right hand,
he catches bitter milk that runs from
the world's wounds and drinks it down
quickly. Curled in fetal sleep inside one egg
among hundreds, a salamander hums as her cells
multiply. The Buddha simply whistles along.
No surprise to find him in the garden tonight,
up to his wrists in wet earth, among pistils
and stamens, an intricate cloud pattern
draping his loins. In the sky, bruised colors
collide. Seeds disperse on the wind while
snails mate in mud from yesterday's rains.

Katya Giritsky

9 Verses, 3 Lines Each, On Baseball

like summertime in childhood
hot pavements in long twilights
the golden voice of baseball on the radio

the cadence that flowed
with the movement of the ball
high and away

and always pulling back to the center
to the diamond in the center
back to home

as we'd be driving home
listening to the ballgame on the radio
driving down mountain switchbacks

in the abrupt fall twilight
sudden appearance of stars
to the roar of stadium noise

fading in and out
as the road twists down the mountain
into the scorching fall night

the promise of winter
the promise of spring still to come
and then summer again and again baseball

and again the golden voice
in the darkness recalling childhood
and heavy canvas covered porch swings

and old men smoking cigars in the twilight
their glowing cigar tips a pulsing beacon in the darkness
pulling in the voice from the radio

Jennifer Goldman

Hockey is Overrated

Oh Montreal—
       Your winter skies are the color of hypothermia,
       your winds sneeze like my grandfather.

       I suppose now I will need to learn to tie a scarf correctly.

       The scarf is consanguineous with the noose,
       whose family tree limbs are bent with the gravity
       of all those hung from them in winters of the
       Grand Wizard sort.

Snot saturated tissues cascade onto the floor
       as incessantly as snowflakes.

       My brain has liquefied, and is dripping from my nostrils.
       I know this is true because I forget each thought
       as quickly as single pieces of confetti
       in a parade.

The snow banks encourage drug binges,
       but refuse to grant me any loans, and so
       my month's shopping list consists of:
              coke,hash,weed,mescaline,mdma,mushrooms,booze,beer,eggs,bread,milk,
              pasta,cannedsauce,concentratedjuice,vitaminB,ecinacea,zinc,ginsing,
       and 31 packs of cigarettes…

       I've smoked so much in here
       my bedroom walls have turned the color of
       morning-after-real-drunk pee.
       The air is the color of cannon balls in flight.

I'm pretty sure I have shrapnel in my lungs.

       Each morning I turn the air purifier on
       to filter a day's worth of smoke from my room.

       I wish I could find a similar device
       for the clearing of clouds
       from my head.

I feel like a frozen wishing well:
    even an optimist would admit I'm defunct.

    Now I know I'm not special.
    So, I have appointed the existential my captain,
    and have set sail for self amusement.

    I wear the deck-swabbing bucket on my head
    to avoid accidentally kicking it.

    I wear my stomach on my sleeve
    to avoid accidentally losing it.

    I know now that idealism is a warm weather sport,
    but baseball season starts soon.

Liz González

September Reds
        for Rachel

His smile is shelved
in the medicine cabinet
beside a bottle of morphine tablets
which no longer muffle his pain

Hours trickle through a tube
His mind rambles, stops on a thought
then spins 100 warped syllables:
he hasn't raked the leaves in weeks,
a memo to Gruber & Glickstein
Will not return to the office

One lung can't expand enough
to let the death sounds loose
He hates the chit-chat of visitors
the human bedposts' rerun of
How do you feel?
He feels like shit

Outside the window,
a collage of red and orange
bursts into hummingbird wings
They lift him out of the rented
hospital bed, up the stairs
and tuck him in his wife's arms

He doesn't want to die
just yet
        just soon

Rafael Jesús González

Calli: House

(definition in the Nahua mode)

It is of carved space
space is defined
       it snarls
       it hums
       it sings
       it is silent.

Our hearts
ephemeral as the flowers
envy them roots;
       in a house
       we pretend to roots.
       We say:
       in this space we live
       here our sleeping is housed.

Beware the house that snarls;
     it will devour you alive.
If you cannot find a house that sings,
     find one that hums.
A house that is silent
must be taught song—
       it is a difficult task;
       one must be certain
       he is a master of song;
       only with a heart of jade
       can we teach our spaces to sing.

Calli: Casa

(definición al modo Nahua)

Es de espacio labrado
se define el espacio
       gruñe
       canturrea
       canta
       calla.

Nuestros corazones
fugaces como las flores
les envidian raíces:
      en una casa
      pretendemos raíces.

      Decimos:
            en este espacio
            vivimos;
            aquí habita
            nuestro dormir.

Teme la casa que gruña;
    te devorará vivo.
Si no encuentras casa que cante,
    encuentra casa que canturree.
Una casa callada
    se tiene que enseñar a cantar—
        es difícil labor:
    Uno se tiene que ser seguro
    que sea maestro del canto;
    solamente con un corazón de jade
    podremos enseñar
    a nuestros espacios cantar.

Jack Grapes

Teaching the Angels

I'll miss Sundays after I'm dead.
I'll miss all the days, I suppose.
Summers especially, the idea of vacation, the whole family
packed in
the car, my mother yelling, "Leave your brother
alone or we're stopping this car this minute and we'll sit
here all day if we have to and you'll never get to Miami
and nobody's going swimming!" Outside, the Everglades,
nothing but cypress trees and alligators.
Christmas I'll miss too. The lights on the tree, and the Chanukah
candles burning on the table.
I'll miss it all. I won't get to read in the paper who won the
ball game,
how the Dodgers are doing, who won the big fight, will
the quarterback throw that last pass to win the game
before he quits forever. Not much sports in Heaven.
Angels—7
New Arrivals—1
Not very competitive.
No one'll write poetry up there, either. What's to write about?
Bliss. Peace. Oneness.
Not exactly themes you can sink your teeth into.
I could always teach the angels how to write.
"Write like you talk."
"We don't need to talk."
"Okay, follow the transformation line."
"We've already transformed. There's nothing to follow."
"Right, Okay. Just give me image and moment."
"That's all there is," they'll say. "The world comes, stays a
moment, then goes away. Image. Moment."
"All right. How about things? No ideas but in things. William
Carlos Williams, a very famous poet, said that."
"Oh, him. He changed his mind. He says it's the other way
around. He's sleeping over there, in that car. Besides, there are
no things here. Just ideas."
I look over at the car. It looks familiar—a gray '47 Dodge.
Sure enough, there's Williams, in the back seat, sitting up,
sleeping.
"Okay," I say, "just tell a story. A simple story."
"I thought this was a poetry class. Now you want stories."
"Look, a poem, a story, it's all the same thing. Writing's
writing."

Now the angels exchange glances. They want a refund.
"Christ!" I say.
"He's in the car with Williams, in the front seat."
Sure enough, there he is, hands resting on the steering wheel.
Beautiful, long fingers.
"Hey, that's my father's car!"
"Of course," they say, "It's your heaven."

Yes, I'll look down and miss it all.
All the things. All the talk.
All the transformations.
I'll miss sitting in the kitchen, watching the cars go by
on Orlando. Josh, coloring a picture on the floor, industriously
snapping the caps back on the markers; Lori, in her robe
reading a book, slurping her coffee; and me, writing this down,
finishing this poem,
returning to the world I so dearly love.

Dina Hardy

Stitching Up the Past

> *El mundo es un pañuelo,* "It's a small world." *Spanish, Lit:*
> *'The world is a handkerchief.' Grooved pie, pt. v. slang, to leave*

The past is a handkerchief he irons, folds four times,
then tucks into his breast pocket. Hours-old coffee
varnishes his tongue as he swigs. Constant humming
from the fish tank. By the door, a cat sleeps
nose open to the threshold, the smell of wet earth.
Outside, rain dances like oil on a fajita skillet.

He pats down the lump of fabric over his heart, feels
picket fences and lemonade on a day hotter than this one,
perched on a porch swing, on Spencer Avenue
in Batchelor, Louisiana, about to pop the question
to Sharon Barron. That was a beautiful day. That was
the worst day of his life, but in captivity, goldfish stop growing
when they reach four inches. They expand three-fold
if they can escape domestication. Really, it was a relief
she said *No.* So, he grooved pie out of the south and settled west
because that's where the sun sleeps and he needed the light.
Mira, chico, there was nothing left to do but buy a bible.

Blind eyes of time, thick with cataracts and the sharp focus
that comes with news that your first love has died. He feeds
the fish with memories, turns the cat to air, leaves,
and crosses paths with Diana, his neighbor,
who was Sharon's best friend in college,
because after all, it is a small world. She was the one
who broke the news to him this morning, now declares,
Any doubts you may have will disappear
early next month, as if this cardboard wisdom
will transform the pain into linen.

El mundo es un pañuelo, he thinks. His car embraces him
while the rain plays jazz on the windshield.
The corners of his world have been unraveling for awhile,
until now, he convinces himself, now as he weaves
into rush hour traffic to retrace the creases of the last forty years.

John C. Harrell

Drops

During some season
It rained
Each afternoon.
Hot steaming drops.

When the helicopters came
Drops of blood
Made beautiful mosaics
In the puddles.
Swirling, mixing
No two pools ever the same.
Some dark pomegranate
Some peppermint
Moving, changing.
Each man's blood blending
With his friends'
And foes'.

Barbara Hauk

Birds In Mid-Air

We are in love,
a party of only two.
We sing naked harmonies
and fly together blind.
I think I am a bird.

Instead, I wake up
in an airplane.
The pilot has taken up
his microphone
to tell all the dirty jokes
he knows.

Two nuns watch
in-flight movies, chins
lifted as if by the same
string. Honeymooners
have their first fight:
he pulls out handfuls
of her hair, she cries.
Nobody pays attention.

You sit next to me:
you speak to me
with other people
in your voice.
My scream can't
compare with
the thunderous whine
of the jet's shaking
aluminum shell.

I rise, not hearing, not seeing,
an automaton of soft parts.
I break open the door,
step out into the empty air.

The last thing I see
is the swarm of birds
covering the plane,
fastened tight.

Jerry Hicks

Blackout

In January 1942 I was five
    on a farm
    outside Los Angeles.

At night,
    it had to be pitch dark
    —like in a closet—
so Jap airplanes couldn't find
    and bomb us.

I didn't know what a "Jap" was
    until one day
    soldiers with rifles
    in a big truck came
and took away our neighbors—
    and sobbing kids.

Where did they keep their planes?
    I wondered.

A tractor and plow in the
    dark field rust'd, and
    all their celery and onions died.

Marvin R. Hiemstra

First

plum blossom petal to escape
dots the velvet brow
of a dog-tired tomcat
dozing in our garden,
dreaming he is
Buddha.

Larkin Higgins

Artist Retreat

Seems idyllic. But these water lilies
must work too. Open at sunrise. Close
at dusk. Open close. Open close.
And on time. How do they keep their
strength up? No bones to count on. Yet
they reveal themselves sunny-side up
like fried eggs every morning.

There is nothing of my regular life here
—except mosquitoes. Koi do not glide
underneath lily pads. Dragonflies do not
abound in my backyard. There is
merely congestion in my helicoptered
sky. The dragonflies would be jealous
of those whirlybirds zooming higher than
their imaginations could grasp.
Much safer flitting closer to the ground.
Or are they? And aren't they tired
beating cellophane wings hundreds of times
per minute? Up down. Up down.
They must have the tiniest of all hinges.
Wings that disappear with speed.

At this temporary home, my heart
is safe. It works hard too, squeezing.
In out. In out. Gives me a queasy
feeling, imagining this muscle. My own
electric charge. Better keep the battery
maintained. Needs strength
for entrances, exits—and you, my dear.

Donna Hilbert

Six Genre

Novel

Anna under the train,
Emma's apothecary poison,
and my late-twentieth century
life meanders, lacks plot.
Character and conflict
appear in abundance and on cue,
but I shrink from the climax,
not wanting the denouement
to occur without me.

Short Story

It's true. The end
and beginning are hard,
but in between is bliss—
the gold coin of revelation—
with no further chapter
in which the piper appears
demanding to be paid
for the unconsidered slap,
the awful kiss.

Poem

I throw my shoulder
out of socket hurtling
lightning from the dark,
portentous clouds.
It's not enough
to touch the gods,
I want to be one.
I think I am, in fact,
levitating here with you,
while below us
children cry
and want their supper.

Movie

In this re-make
the plot is hackneyed
but well-wrought
and the star turns reverse for twist:
she refuses to leave her husband
while he fears he's just an object used
for sex.
Distraught, she tumbles
from plot point to plot point
praying *deus ex machina*
save me. Save me.

Play

Better to rise and fall
in one act.

Problems with the second
are classic:
everyone onstage to explain—
no ecstasy, all exposition.

What is sadder than the curtain on act three?
Extra time, to be sure,
but we fall on the sword
just the same.

Opera

Every night while I cook dinner
Mimi dies
in grand voice, consumptive
under a blood-spumed Paris moon.

How can there be more suffering than this?

Every night to die for passion,
yet be forced alive
assigned the living task of chopping onion,
smashing buds of garlic with a spoon.

Marilyn Hochheiser

Woman, Eighty, Stranded In Desert Dies

No,
I wouldn't want to go
that way

bogged down in deep sand
one-half mile
off the crossroads

but, maybe, that's
how we all leave
the earth

vulnerable as a rabbit

our high-pitched cries
piercing the infinite sky
like arrows.

Nancy Hom

Bread and Soup

Beneath the bare bulb
we gather to eat our evening meal
of bread and soup. Here behind the
mission walls the kind priest
speaks to us in euphemisms.
He avoids staring at our brown roasted faces,
our hardboiled hands, our violet veins.
He mouths his words like a fish,
careful not to mention China to us,
who are now fatherless and motherless
in this new country.

He does not know that
we have created our own miracle
that has transformed the stale hard crust
into crisp crackling pork skin;
the zucchini soup into
the finest winter melon broth.
Our lips, puckered by pungent memories,
smack in satisfaction at this,
our only taste of home.

Jodi L. Hottel

Shikata ga nai

Shikata ga nai
means
It can't be helped

which translates
scour and scrub
till the smell of horse urine
is a faint memory,
cobble a table out of
scavenged fruit crates,
create a home from the stall
that is temporary shelter for
your family of six.

Pretend you don't see barbed wire
or soldiers with rifles in guard towers
when you gaze at Heart Mountain on the horizon.

Shikata ga nai—
a tacit agreement
to adopt the government jargon:
    relocation and internment
        not concentration or prison camp,

to be as American as possible,
having to prove your loyalty
even though you were born here.

And when your daughter hungers to know
about your life in camp,
you giggle about the "hi-jinks girls"
and being prom queen,
a typical teenage life.

It suggests
your secret, mounting dread
each year as December 7th approaches,
even now, over fifty years later.

Shikata ga nai means
        End of discussion.
        I don't want to talk about it.
        There's nothing more to say.

Robin D. Hudechek

Bird Gathering

As a young girl you fed birds,
imagining their beaks against the crisp bells
in your own palms.
The humming birds are the freest, dipping in sugar water
and hovering just long enough for the sun to flash on their
fat tummies, too heavy for a thing so small.

The doves drop companionably into the food dish
swinging like eager babies
until they are driven away by finches.
You watch the swallows tow a "v" across the sky
and wonder at the beating of wings. Yesterday,
your arms were so light, boneless,
outstretched against a ripple of hills and marsh waters.

It's not so easy keeping the neighbors away
or the gardens with four corners
or cats from prowling below the feeders.
There are fewer birds now, fewer nests
in the spidery leaves of the eucalyptus.

Bucket in hand, you watch
for the black and white cat, and think
as the water splashes his face
your hands are too heavy now, too still.

Sometimes the cat does manage to leap
and descend with flailing wings, then
curl his tail like a coat hanger
and press his sleek back against your legs,
proud of the bird on the porch, proud of the wings
folded against the body and the eyes pressed shut
against the faintest fleck of water.

D'ellen Hutchens

Something Blue
          for Christa

I did not dance at your wedding,
but heard of your union sing-song from half siblings
I would have thought too young
to know such secrets.

I did not toast to your happiness,
as did your father and his new bride,
or your grandparents, the master and mistress
of cheap champagne, where good wishes

have always bubbled forth
as easily as the libation
and where love is measured like liquor—
in quantity, not quality.

I did not hand down the Victorian lace,
packed carefully away all these years
with the hope it would bring
you more luck in love than myself.

No, you wore thermal underwear
under jeans and flannel
as you stood in drifts of snow,
lake-edged, somewhere in New Hampshire—

holding the hand of a boy
one year your junior—
vows supervised by a justice of the peace.
You call, weeks after

to break old news—
your own words crossing to my ear
cold and distant as the east coast blizzard.
Already bundled in your defense

of young love and promises of forever,
you expect my broken heart to issue the standard,
"BUT YOU ARE ONLY 19" lecture.
Your fears are met instead

with unnerving calm and chit-chat,
as I, resolved to let you believe,
recall myself at only 17.
I know you know it all—

no one can tell you different.
Perhaps this is how it's supposed to be,
me, parenting by phone from my desk in California,
discussing the weather

and the spelling of your new name,
while you brace for another cold front,
and I watch hot, devil winds
blow the Los Angeles sky a clear and empty blue.

Elizabeth Iannaci

His first cry

is small and fierce. Suddenly,
I can no longer be trusted with secrets.
Tell me nothing vital—
I would give it up in an instant. Now
there is something in this life
worth ransom.

Victor D. Infante

A Poor Attempt at Eulogy (for Louis)

> "Life is an illusion that we must take seriously"
> —Carl Jung

The story always begins with shattering
and ends with veins alight with fire.

You, young and tossing emptied bottles down cliffs.
You, delighting in the symphony
of gravity and broken glass.

In the time it takes to walk from Aramea to India and back
you lived a lifetime. *The Buddha returned as Albert Einstein,*
tried to be concise this time, but the wind was dry
and underneath parched lips we spit cartoons,
penned scandal sheets
elected someone president.

There is no name for your passing,
no consciousness of you for years except slight mentions.
Your death was one of twenty-seven e-mails.
I almost deleted it unread. *Consider*
the television as Delphi: four years like clockwork
when the dead arise and claim the Kingdom
for their poor, shallow saviors.

Our leaders would be comic book heroes.
You were almost real, and I have barely voice to whisper prayers.
No thought of you for years, and now your absence stings
like the needles puncturing your arm,
burns in my throat like carcinogen.

In the time it takes to walk the empty distance between us
countries fell and were reborn. The world progressed,
and somehow what was dead and meaningless
we took too seriously.

You have become apocrypha, the blank religion of sleight of hand.
Jesus returned as Harry Houdini.
Tried to explain that he was never in the box at all.

Larry Jaffe

Hoopster

It all started on the playground
shooting hoops with friends.

There were five Larry's
in our neighborhood,
and when one mama shouted Larry
all five commenced to running.

Then there was the morning
three of us awaited
the High School bus.

We played horse
a basketball game
of ghostlike pretensions
winner takes all
to the next morning contest.

We aimed potshots at the basket
without acclaim a
time passing ritual.

Suddenly!
Larry Mohlman shouted
at Larry Kempster:
*"You're just like a Jew
you can only do one thing!"*
Because he kept shooting lay-ups,
was not basketball worldly and wise,
did not diversify his shots
and kept driving persistence
to the backboard.

I looked on in disbelief
just as suddenly realizing why Molhman
always picked on me since age of six.

So with hook shot in hand,
set shot from perimeter,
jump shot from downtown
this Larry
meaning Jaffe

asked that Larry
meaning Mohlman
if I shot just like a Jew too.

He did not answer
turning red as his hair
as I proceeded to
take him to the cleaners
while all I could think
about were showers.

Dale Jensen

Predictions 2003

in the   coming   new   age
            a country in south America will suffer psychics especially in europe
            the stock market will consider the tabloids as a pregnancy rumor
            very small dogs will wear diamond rings with youth and so are gloves
            soccer will win the super bowl   stem cell research will win the world series
            the pope meets with a prime television slot and the scene out of east bedlam
            a large portrait of ronald reagan will stay in the media spotlight as another
            relationship scandal
            flooding in january creates a power plant disaster and volcanic activity erupts
            in the world's citizens

wear colors that make you feel good
            wear any color you like   summer or winter personally
            yellow adrenal glands leap at lunch at an expensive restaurant
            oddly walking around healing properties of mice
            in fact a nice blue shirt might give them a needed rest
            it's popular or somebody else   forget it   you're smarter than you think

Rachel Kann

Pretty Talk

Case # 34-263
Intensity vs. dignity.
Dead center of winter.
I testify:

You and I
snuck into the theatre on Christopher street.
(How stupid were they to give us both our own set of keys?)
After drinking ourselves silly at the back fence;
you, on cold-buffalo-winter-type libations.
Always Rolling Rock/Guinness/JD if you were in a hurry.
I don't remember what I was drinking,
but about you,
I remember everything.

Like the knit cap that said "Dolomite."
Which was from an actual mine
where they actually mined
the actual substance, Dolomite.

You were that cool without even trying.

And I remember your round wire glasses,
and how your last name was a verb and a noun, like mine
and when the bars closed at 4,
fingers freezing and jumpy we'd unlock the theatre door,
plop down right in the lobby and
read our favorite Shepard and Bukowski
to each other,
proud of the sound of how righteous, passionate, loud
our voices could be.

And then when we'd leave,
we'd go back home
to our place in Brooklyn Heights
where we were roommates
always acting like we never expected anything to happen
and when we'd end up in bed
you never had your glasses on,
and you were blind without them.

I used to love staring up into that vacuous cow eye gaze
so oddly placed upon your brilliant face
and always
right after you came
while you were still inside me
you'd put your glasses back on,
blinking me into focus,
and I really liked that,
and…

…you never said you loved me.

God only knows if you ever did.

Case # 17-256
Lust vs. subversiveness
Dead center of summer.
I testify:

You and I
snuck into the walk-in fridge
downstairs in the just-below-Harlem jazz bar we both worked in.

It was too damn hot.
Catching your scent when you went past me,
I'd be wet in a nanosecond.

We couldn't help it!
We collided against racks of zucchini and cabbages
squishing squash
and when my eyes finally shot open to watch the door
I caught sight of the slaughtered lamb
skinned just minutes before
by the hateful Haitian chef I loved more than life—
like a daddy.

Fate had made her my sister by placing her in there.
Rachel, Hebrew for lamb of God
both of us sacrificed on the altar of desire that night
as I took you inside me
and at 4 am when the bar finally closed
we'd both have an after-work drink—
Bacardi Limón and Coke.
(Another thing you taught me.)

We'd squeeze 10 pieces of lemon into each glass
and you'd speak to me in Spanish, and I'd reply in my messed-up Spanish
and then we'd stumble out, turning opposite corners
and I'd ride the 9 train
all the way home.

Alone.

...you told me you loved me about a million times;
God only knows if you ever did.

Case # 26-348

You'd make things so complicated;
I'd get so frustrated
all I could do was cry.

Case # 4-13

You'd scream at me
to stop psychoanalyzing
everything.

2-5
You'd lie
and tell me you were single.

89
You were
terrified of my passion.

7
You'd let me down.

3
You'd stare at me;
a broken heap on the floor
and be at a loss for how to proceed.
It never occurred to you

to hold me.

I'm running in circles.
Looking for a loophole,

trying to be tried for prior uncomprehended crimes
and leave with a scot-free rap sheet this time.

I want to make your obtuse angle bend into spiritual acuity.
Some part of me believes
if I can solve it for you and I
then all these chains would break
and I'd walk out of this prison,
but I find you infinitely compelling
you…
…you emotionally distant *man*!

Your kisses crash instantly
into that rift of what no one can give to me
but
I can't not want it,
and if I could figure out how,

I'd end this poem right now.

Eloise Klein Healy

Oh, Dr. Surgeon

cuidado

because what if my wrist locks in place like a rusty gate and whatever I have in mind can't get through, whatever I try to hold can't catch. What if the hinge there is too old to repair and forever after all my shirts will not tuck right, drying off with a towel will hurt me hurt me, drying my hair will hurt and pulling up the covers hurt and worse, every thing I go to touch will have to be thought through, thought through when there is a vocabulary of impulse

right there in the air at the end of my fingers, stories spun by the little bones in their tiny dance. It is not enough to speak, you know. It is not enough to have the words to say things. There is that moment, you know, when something has to hang in the air. Hang in the air for a moment, and turn

not on the tip of the tongue, the pointed slippery tongue, but here en el dictionario de mis dedos, las palabras huesudos clicking cumulative as a litany, running repetitive and desperate to find a saint still awake to gesture, someone who in the past has worked miracles with the touch of her hand and can still identify with the little needs of the living, a saint of small things like The Little Flower, who understands dusting and folding, who probably hurt herself and dipped her hand in Holy Water or cried out just a little and then only in private

if I could pray anymore I would return to the rosary because it is filled with wood and jewels, because I carried my grandmother's in my pocket like a talisman for years, because even with a simple string you can make one if both your hands work, because when I can't sleep I can repeat the prayers attached to suffering, to joy, to memory, to the blessedness of what comes around again, familiar and whole.

Ron Koertge

1989

Because AIDS was slaughtering people left and right,
    I went to a lot of memorial services that year.
There were so many, I'd pencil them in between
    a movie or a sale at Macy's. The other thing that
made them tolerable was the funny stories people
    got up and told about the deceased: the time he
hurled a mushroom frittata across a crowded room,
    those green huraches he refused to throw away,
the joke about the flight attendant and the banana
    that cracked him up every time.

But this funeral was for a blind friend of my wife's
    who'd merely died. And the interesting thing
about it was the guide dogs; with all the harness
    and the sniffing around, the vestibule of the church
looked like the starting line of the Iditarod. But
    nobody got up to talk. We just sat there
and the pastor read the King James version. Then he
    said someday we would see Robert and he us.

Throughout the service, the dogs slumped beside their
    masters. But when the soloist stood and launched
into a screechy rendition of *Abide With Me*, they sank
    into the carpet. A few put their paws over their ears.
Someone whispered to one of the blind guys; he told
    another, and the laughter started to spread. People
in the back looked around, startled and embarrassed,
    until they spotted all those chunky Labradors
flattened out like animals in a cartoon about
    steamrollers. Then they started too.

That was more like it. That was what I was used to:
a roomful of people laughing and crying, taking off
their sunglasses to blot their inconsolable eyes.

Paradise Lost

Westlake Memorial Cemetery is bordered
on the north by busy Route 157, but sometimes
a deer steps out of the trees south of plot 272,
nibbles from a mound, then darts away.

I only get back here once a year or so, so I see
how the toys on the graves of the children change:
Power Rangers replace Ninja Turtles. Red Camaros
are crushed by Widow Maker Monster Trucks.
And the cemetery changes, too, slowly moving west
in the measured tread of progress.

Today, a young poet has slipped his jacket over
the back of my father's grave as if he were saving
someone a seat in assembly. I know he's a poet
because he has a fancy notebook and he wears
his loneliness like a beret.

It says in the Bible that where two or three
poets are gathered together, they tend to form
a circle and nod sympathetically. But this one
is alone, and he scowls at me.

So I stroll to the edge of the bluff where even
the dead will have to stop. A breeze off
the Mississippi turns the page of the evening.
A thousand cicadas sound like Milton
ranting at his daughters.

Judy Z. Kronenfeld

Names of My Mother's Friends

They touched knees on stoops, girlishly
coquettish, hung laundry together
on wind-scoured roofs, smiled at me
fit to burst, her *naches* theirs, yahooed hello
as I dragged home from school, pinched
my cheeks red because they loved her,
removed slipcovers at the end
of summer, lovingly preserved grandmothers'
antimacassars, leaned on the sills
of evening.

              They rumbled their shopping carts
over cracked sidewalks, met in the
vegetable store by the dank potatoes,
cluck-clucked over this one's
sunken-cheeked husband, that one's
sneaky son, while the chickens
they chose were plucked;
                  grew
widowed, cancerous, forgot which was
the meat fork, which the dairy,
lost teeth and didn't care, moved
out of and into a home,
              and their
names have been sent down to the dark,
withdrawn from circulation, with hers
they have gone out like lights,
but they are still fragrant
as lace handkerchiefs taken
from a sachet-scented drawer—
Oh Stella, Dora, Ida, Gertie, Pearl, oh Rose.

naches = Yiddish for a proud pleasure or joy, especially one that comes from
the accomplishments of a child.

Beverly Lafontaine

Musicale

The sun is the accompanist this afternoon.
Heat tongues the underbelly of leaves.
Musicians linger in their screened room,
instruments grasped and stroked like lovers.

Heat tongues the underbelly of leaves.
Adobe walls throb to the strains of
instruments grasped and stroked like lovers.
Restless for the adulation of strangers,

adobe walls throb to the strains of
silk and leather fondled to a sheen.
Restless for the adulation of strangers,
women loop pearls of tears 'round iridescent fingers.

Silk and leather fondled to a sheen
flaunt their shadow-play while impatient
women loop pearls of tears 'round iridescent fingers.
Against the dauntless sky black birds

flaunt their shadow-play while impatient
lovers press tongues to swollen lips.
Against the dauntless sky black birds
soar in an adagio for summer as

lovers press tongues to swollen lips.
The sun, the accompanist this afternoon,
soars in an adagio for summer as
musicians linger in their screened room.

Robert Lanphar

Beached Whales

The Winnabegos lined up
Diesel pushers, pullers
Dual AC, side out expansions
Generators, automatic hydraulic jacks
Satellite dishes.

These 30-40 foot monsters
Alive with the sharing that
Five families bring
Each Mother's Day weekend.
Many in the pod have
Moved on to more appropriate grounds.
Somehow the annual call
Keeps bringing them back
For one more season.

Cheryl Latif

Inside Out

come spring, you abandon the garden
cling to reasons for moving past this breath.

my gaze wanders to a cobweb in the corner,
i can't say how long it has been there.

outside the wind is a frantic heart.
inside, the air, still as death.

Viet Le

The Edge of the World

Your life of seventeen years becomes miniature
        from the plane window:
        graffiti on fences,
the Monroe High School field like a straw mat,
the K-mart where I work (a checkout lady, who would've thought),
cardboard strip malls;
        suburban boxes, capillary highways
                contracts, expands like your breath against the glass.

My daughter, the orb of your eye
        mirrors the edge of the world.

I imagine
        what your dorm will look like—
                worn hardwood floors, chipped plaster walls.

Below us, a confusion of sky and foam,
the ocean bursting white.

Crossing an ink sea
        thirty years ago (my only other flight)
from another country;
        grasping your father's rough hands, dark as Bodhi tree roots,
                huddled in rags from the Thai refugee camp,
                        certain only of the watery moon.

Landing in America for the first time at night—
        a country ablaze,
                        an exodus of fireflies.

Cricket Lee

Mental Patterns: Two Alleys

I.

The alleyways in Belmont
lined with bushes
sprouting flowers in Spring,
are as foreign to me as
Emporio Armani
and Pierre Cardin.

On one side of the hedge
long homes, multi-colored
with different motifs
have sprouted from the ground—
a miniature replica of Melrose.

On the other side
fresh paint covers blemishes
and scars on old buildings
where fresh lattes are being brewed,
photographs being enlarged,
parents painting pottery
with their children and
pancakes served—
the smell of maple syrup
slipping through the cracks
of the Shore House Café.

II.

In the alleys of my youth
old newspapers and brown
paper sacks soaked into
the water left standing from rain
and indiscriminate hoses.

Leftover shards from broken
bottles congregated among
the chain link
separating the bums
from the abused church
and apartments of practitioners.

Our parents warned us of these
mini roadways, walkway of fiends.

On rebellious days we rode
our scooters through the grime,
speeding past the curb side preachers—
the port princes
only to end up
on the other side of nowhere
preparing for the long way home,
too scared to press our luck
twice in one day.

Stellasue Lee

Without Looking Back

She walks from the terminal,
enters the movable corridor
toward the plane, which waits.

Reaching the end, she will step up,
a small step that will lead
into the cabin of the jet,
the one that will carry her

to a city entirely unknown to her.
In the time it takes,
she will have reinvented herself,
changed her lipstick from soft mauve

to Firecracker Red, and placed a scarf
around her shoulders drenched in perfume
something light and carefree,
that will flutter in the late afternoon breeze—

She will look for her assigned seat
reading the numbers posted
below the overhead compartments
until her number, the one that matches

the ticket she holds in her hand
appears, and it will be then she sees the man
already seated, and will stop, smile,
and when he looks up to meet her gaze

she will notice his mouth drop open
slightly as he unsnaps his seat belt,
moving quickly now, to allow himself
to unfurl from where he has been sitting.

She will step back, allow him to enter the aisle
before taking her place at the window.
Already her new life has begun,
no longer a secretary, or teacher, or receptionist,

but the life she has created,
the one that is fitting for a woman
wearing Fircracker Red lipstick,
drenched in a fragrance called Interlude.

Carol Lem

My *Life*
(*after Billy Collins*)

Sometimes I see it as college ruled
line paper with black ballpoint ink
writing up the day's course

or as incense smoke circling
then disappearing into a blue lamp.

When the telephone invades my room
or a gunmetal sky hovers
and I don't know whether to stay in or out

it is a ping pong ball,
a sparring between rubber paddles
with no one to keep score
except the old woman
with failing eyes and memory.

So here in these dusty corridors
it is a house with many doors, the keys
lost in this one room
I've been looking for poem after poem.

Sometimes, like dreams, it is a city,
a labyrinth of streets,
signs pulling me this way and that
until at last I wake to my cat
perched by the window eyeing a bird

or to a car starting up another day,
and in the next two hours
it is a fountain of ink flowing out
slamming gates, screams, and trains.

But at the moment, imitating stanzas,
looking at his page and then mine,
candle flame and cello to find a line for,

I am a flute, my sound is an empty bell,
and my life is *chikudo*, the bamboo way,
shaping everything into a musical phrase—

falling leaves, rain dripping from eaves,
white rocks scattered across the roof top,
even the boy skateboarding by.

Philip Levine

The Simple Truth

I bought a dollar and a half's worth of small red potatoes,
took them home, boiled them in their jackets
and ate them for dinner with a little butter and salt.
Then I walked through the dried fields
on the edge of town. In middle June the light
hung on in the dark furrows at my feet,
and in the mountain oaks overhead the birds
were gathering for the night, the jays and mockers
squawking back and forth, the finches still darting
into the dusty light. The woman who sold me
the potatoes was from Poland; she was someone
out of my childhood in a pink spangled sweater and sunglasses
praising the perfection of all her fruits and vegetables
at the road-side stand and urging me to taste
even the pale, raw sweet corn trucked all the way,
she swore, from New Jersey. "Eat, eat," she said,
"Even if you don't I'll say you did."
                                        Some things
you know all your life. They are so simple and true
they must be said without elegance, meter and rhyme,
they must be laid on the table beside the salt shaker,
the glass of water, the absence of light gathering
in the shadows of picture frames, they must be
naked and alone, they must stand for themselves.
My friend Henri and I arrived at this together in 1965
before I went away, before he began to kill himself,
and the two of us to betray our love. Can you taste
what I'm saying? It is onions or potatoes, a pinch
of simple salt, the wealth of melting butter, it is obvious,
it stays in the back of your throat like a truth
you never uttered because the time was always wrong,
it stays there for the rest of your life, unspoken,
made of that dirt we call earth, the metal we call salt,
in a form we have no words for, and you live on it.

Larry Levis

Decrescendo

If there is only one world, it is this one.

In my neighborhood, the ruby-helmeted woodpecker's line
Is all spondees, & totally formal as it tattoos
Its instinct & solitude into a high sycamore which keeps

Revising autumn until I will look out, &
Something final will be there: a branch in winter—not
Even a self-portrait. Just a thing.

Still, it is strange to live alone, to feel something
Rise up, out of the body, against all that is,
By law, falling & turning into the pointless beauty

Of calendars. Think of the one in the office closed
For forty-three summers in a novel by Faulkner, think
Of unlocking it, of ducking your head slightly
And going in. It is all pungent, & lost. Or

It is all like the doomed singers, Cooke & Redding,
Who raised their voices against the horns'
Implacable decrescendos, & knew exactly what they

Were doing, & what they were doing was dangerous.

The man on sax & the other on piano never had to argue
Their point, for their point was time itself; & all
That one wished to say, even to close friends,
One said beside that window: The trees turn; a woman
Passing on the street below turns up her collar against
The cold; &, if the music ends, the needle on the phonograph
Scrapes like someone raking leaves, briefly, across
A sidewalk, & no one alone is, particularly, special.

That is what musicians are for, to remind us of this, unless

Those singers die, one shot in a motel room
By a woman who made a mistake; & one dead
In a plane crash, an accident.

Which left a man on sax & another on piano
With no one to back up, &, hearing the news,

One sat with his horn in a basement in Palo Alto,
Letting its violence go all the way up, &
Annoying the neighbors until the police came,
And arrested him—who had, in fact, tears
In his eyes. And the other, a white studio
Musician from L.A., who went home & tried

To cleave the keyboard with his hands until
They bled, & his friends came, & called his wife,
And someone went out for bandages & more bourbon—
Hoping to fix up, a little, this world.

Carol Ann Lindsay

For My Girl Who Died Too Young

I save my tears when they say
your body mangled in a car wreck
may not breathe tomorrow,
because you are a survivor.
Then, I let masked men take you
into the polished cathedral,
for expensive tatoos that run
from your throat all the way down.
You would savor the crooked design
conceived in a season cursed
with sleepless nights, sterile smells,
and "code blue" bells.

*

I watch the bed waiting,
(on the day of the Spring equinox,
when our hills are green
from winter rain) and expect you,
my miracle child,
to wake up and say, "Surprise."
Each second is eternity,
every minute, brutal time,
while acid pain inside of me
is fertilized by reality
when I learn what you knew
about the brain,
that it's the hard drive
for the mind which is the software
for the soul, which is the user.

*

I can't see the sun through fog
that devours me. I can't sense
time because dreams feast
on phantom flashes of life
when your body sleeps.
Everything you did
is sealed with sweet and sticky sap
to the marrow of my soul.
Everything you said
is caged in my mind

as I try to make the past real
when it isn't, try to make yesterday
alive, while it's dying with your flesh.

*

I think about what I'll give you—
the diamond necklace your father gave
me, crystal glasses in the china closet,
and my mother's silver star ring
that you took from my dresser
last year. But I feel you over me,
laughing, and I know it's ridiculous
to think of these things
when you aren't really dying, just
changing spaces the way salmon swim
and find the sea before returning upstream
to spawn and start the cycle of life again.

*

My tears grow fierce like a desert storm
the second your spirit is free. I am weak
from the poisonous plague
that steals a slice of my soul
with creation's climax.

*

The way we were and the way it
was with you, my blue-eyed blond,
lives as a brief breath in eternity
now that you are gone.

*

Today I envy ten years ago,
when life hungered
for free space and future.
If I could only stand in the rain
and let it rinse away
this swollen Spring, I would
surrender to the miracles
of incarnated days
when there wasn't time.
I would capture every second
and I wouldn't think about tomorrow

or dust and dirty dishes. I would choke
life with my love and learn each one
of those dumb blond jokes you told me
rather than be seduced by poetry.

*

From your bedroom I hear
the eerie whine under a full moon
and remember Felix, your cat
disappeared so that
coyotes could celebrate lunch.
I see night decorated
with empty shadows that loom
over your marble Buddha
and Nirvana poster. I wonder
if your last words to me,
"I love you too," will fade
with the dress I caress. I feel
the hollow spot and close the door
to a living tomb that silently sears
                         —my heart forever.

For Candice A. Lindsay — September 5, 1980-May 22, 1997

J.D. Lloyd

Pleiades

1.
Mother touches my elbow, tugs
      me from the hall to her dresser.
She opens the flat cherry box on top
      and pulls out a ring I've never seen,
the one she took off when Daddy left,
      when I was just a tickle in her belly.
Seven diamonds—dewdrops sprinkled
      on the gold-leaf petals of a rose.
She nods toward my girlfriend sitting
      in the den, says "I want you to use
these stones in her engagement ring."

2.
I re-set them six in a circle, orbiting
      a raised solitaire. One diamond
for each good year of our marriage—
      a flawless little system of light
burning itself out on her finger.

Two weeks into the separation
      she calls from her mother's house.
She's lost it—can't imagine where.
      I hang up envisioning her hands
clawing at wet sheets, the ring waiting
      in a fold for the maid at a Motel 6.

3.
I climb the stairs to my bachelor, find
      five glass window louvers stacked
against the stucco wall—inside,
      my jewelry box empty on the floor.

The officer writes *gold wedding band*
      beneath VCR and *compact discs,*
slaps his folder shut. I walk with him
      to the cruiser and continue down Venice
to the beach. Free of the streetlights,
      I look up, search the night sky until
I locate the Seven Sisters. And I imagine
      my mother, even my ex-wife, eyes
upturned to that small setting of stars.

Victoria Locke

Making Love to Einstein

Albert,
either you were born too soon
or I too late
to run my fingers through your crazy hair.
Genius warmth against my skin.

One morning you'd wake me and
explain for the first time that bend in space
and when the grey glass brightened,
your dark eyes would say,
"Don't ever leave me."

We'd drink the best wine,
we'd travel
and if you leaned across the table and said,
"Gravity cannot be held responsible for people falling in love."
I wouldn't laugh.

I'm wise enough to know
I have needed you my whole life.
Our sparkling bonfire
brilliant in my mind.

Gerald Locklin

the impresario

i show up at ferrara's ristorante
about two fifty-five in order to
take advantage of the luncheon menu
which is such a good deal,
especially the linguini pescatore,
with bread, soup or salad, and beverage
for $11.95. at this time of day
i'm the only customer, but joe ferrara
makes sure the staff makes me feel welcome,
even if i'm interrupting their preparations
for the dinner hour. and joe ferrara is
always there! today he is personally
slicing the fresh bell peppers at a table
by the door. otherwise he would pull up
a chair with me, address me as professor,
ask about today's students, deplore
the decline in standards, in pride, in
just about everything, most especially
the food service industry. and today,
as i'm leaving, he has finished with the
peppers and is putting together some
coleman heaters, reflectors, and patio
fixtures that he picked up at a going-out-
of-business sale. that will allow him to
hold down the cost of my pescatore.

the cooking is always as superb as
the service...because joe oversees both,
fixing his own special tomato and onion salad,
monitoring the sautés,
dining mainly on his own cuisine
because it really is the best around.
needless to say he personally shops for
the fish, meats, produce,
the imported oils and wines.

so, you want to have the best restaurant in
town? the recipe is simple:
do everything yourself,
love your job, enjoy your customers,
be tough enough not to tolerate a slackening
of effort from your staff or of quality

from your purveyors,
don't get greedy,

and be convinced in the fibre of your being
that feeding people well is no less
a command performance than a production of *aida*.

sequence of reactions to south park

first, it makes me laugh out loud.

then, i shake my head at what's
allowed these days on television.

next, i begin to wonder if our
society has not in fact sunk somewhere
beneath the level of gomorrha.

eventually it dawns on me that
what i'm watching bears a lot in
common with certain early works
of my own.

Suzanne Lummis

White Dress

Even then I knew what I didn't want: all this.
The tiny pair in formal dress pressed
stiffly on the cake gazed toward
some future which left their faces blank.
The descent of creamy roses underneath
them looked like dreams. They seemed
like incidentals in some melting grand design.

But maybe I was just one too!
My pink dress poofed around my knees,
I couldn't press it flat. On the table,
on a stack, I saw my parents gift,
a hand-carved birdhouse painted white
and blue. The boring Mertons brought
a set of steak knifes looking out
the window of a box, through cellophane.
My parents were a married couple, too,
but not like that. Still,
I knew how marriage worked, I'd seen TV.
I wouldn't have it, a house with someone
always in it, his presence there
even when he was out, taking its place
at the head of the table or behind
a newspaper in the biggest, softest chair.

The bride made her rounds as if awake
inside a dream, then leaned—half swooned
I thought—toward me. Her veil swept around
me like a net, or cornucopia that spilled
the sudden gift of sight. I caught
her gardenia scent, and the silk
along her neck sowed with tiny pearls, seeds
about to hatch. A burst
of dandelions would make the air fly white.
The wine I'd sipped made me feel faint,
lathed by pearl, the rush of dry
fine lace—as if man and woman, now
and ever, had fallen from the sky,
omniscient, personal and lush.

"Darling you look lovely!" said the face.
Then the mystery of union let me go, tossed me
back into what I was before, and drifted on.

Short Poem Demanding Massive Social Action

I wake up, my cold is gone. Already
my cats are darting about with polite
expressions on their faces, pursuing
their humble lives.
The wine glasses from last night's party
rise from here, there, a sort
of shimmering in the room
like the presence of imagination.
Someone built these castles in the air
then couldn't break the spell.
Something hums with desire and possibility.
People, why keep blaming the world
when the world is this full?
Fling open your windows.
Throw out the old way of thinking.

Glenna Luschei

A Pereira

We hit it right, driving back from Fresno,
cattle wading through green. Grass parted
like oceans through Portuguese dairy farms,

horses forged like horseshoes into mountains.
Good luck all the way! We picnicked in wild-
flowers, faces remembered, names forgotten.

With their fragrance it all came back:
Blue-eyed grass, Cup o' Gold, Clarkia. A stop
at the James Dean monument in Chalome

to consider the inscription: *The young who fall
as blossoms are eternal.* Nearby a biker
with a leather jacket that read, "Jesus

would have rode a Harley." At home, a drift
of pear blossoms greeted me. My *Pereira*
bloomed while I was gone.

O, let me have another passionate chance.

Alison Luterman

Another Vigil at San Quentin

Not quite midnight. My candle stutters
under the half-full moon, the frightened stars.

Someday in the future, people will be curious
about these rituals: how
we murdered them at dead of night, strapped to beds,
poison injections dripping, scientifically timed,
thinking ourselves modern.

And some of us, the lecturer will explain,
dressed up like guards
(two rows of them here, visors
pushed back, batons at the ready),
and some like newsmen, clambering over low rooftops
with their kleig lights and cameras.
And the rest of us drabs, like weary and defiant protesters,
arm in arm, with our candles and sage

and We Shall Overcome and in this case eagle feathers,
as the accused killer
(all right, he really did it)
is a Native American, who
(if you want the whole story)
lured a girl-child to his car,
raped, sodomized her—go on, tell it—stripped and flung
this ten-year-old from a bridge
into a gully, as if she were a beer can he'd just crushed
under his heel, and left for litter.

Say that part. And then, to enact
our rage, express our unspeakable
horror at the ravage of our daughter,
we'll carefully poison him.
The candles burn down.
The counter-protesters,
Christians to a man, get on their megaphone.
"Ten minutes to repent! Nine more minutes
or your soul will burn!
Eight minutes and the Lord is your judge!"

Our songs pick up as well; We Shall Not
We Shall Not Be Moved,

Gonna Lay Down My Sword and Shield,
and a Navajo chant.
The current swells. Inside,
a frightened, screwed-up
man is being prepared for death and burial.
He has requested that a medicine man, with sage,
accompany him in his death chamber. Request denied.

All right, one eagle feather,
to be pinned to the sheet over his body.
I link arms with the rough wool coat
next to me, bow my head into a friend's shoulder,
thinking about my own rape
at the hands of a rageful drunk, years ago.

I don't have words
for what I'm doing here, only the smell
of the ocean going on and on below us,
crash, smash, gotcha.
And the softness of the air on my cheeks,
and the sound of screaming gulls.
Last week the rains finally stopped.
The peach tree is in full pink flower.
Earth seems to have forgiven
our uncountable human sins again
and opened her arms to us in Spring. O pure

right and wrong, how I long for you.
Tell the people of the future I came here for confusion
and ignorance and darkness.
For the white lick of flame against the char of ash.
For poison and reason and the old moon,
and a stubborn idea about the innocence of things,
and for the smell of candle wax
dripping silently and slowly.

Full Moon

The men on Alameda Beach
are pulling striped bass from the glittering water.
Small red stars of cigarettes between their fingers.
Poles stationed like sentinels, stuck in the sand,
lines cast far out,
buckets at the ready.
Waves wash over the tired shoreline
like a lace slip over bare brown shoulders.
The men grin to each other, don't say much.
Fish flop in the pail. Sand dabs. Bass.
The bay is full of dioxin; do they know?
They are fishing to feed their families
in a school of different languages: Tagalog,
Hmong, Mien, Spanish, Vietnamese.
In the dark, a man can be a man
or a shadow in the moonlight, voice out of night,
just another kind of animal with two fine, flexible hands.
Each one standing full of private thoughts,
up to his knees in alive water.
Fish know the truth of depth and shimmer,
then the hook and the fatal sparkling air.
The men know what they know
even if tomorrow at the factory, and the next day, and the next,
will press the memory of this freedom
flatter than a glint of mica. Still, it shines.

Bil Luther

Winter Solstice

a lucidly pale blue sky
except in the far west
out beyond Catalina
where a wide curtain
of mare's tail cirrostratus
seems to rise from the cold currents
that flow there
filtering the Sun
like orange gauze.

—

Brilliant wake
follows me
wherever I move
and Catalina
is hazy, but,
more well defined than usual,
humped in the South,
a long low ridge, a short plain,
and, another small ridge to the North

—

She begins to reveal herself
even more clearly as the Sun
becomes a bright variegated glow
behind this now umbering curtain.

—

There will certainly be
no green flash
tonight.

—

Only a huge fading ember
as Catalina
intervenes.

—

As the glow dims
the question is

will the Sun break through
and alert us to that moment of truth
when it is truly almost gone?

—

The mare's tails range
from tightlined streaks
in the far distant North
to the wispy white plumes
here in the South
and closer.

—

A far, far sailor
moves slowly along
the bottom edge of the island
while gulls and swallows
wheel
in their final parade.

—

The Sun
has just now
passed below
and sharply behind
the bottom of the curtain
and the top of the sea
while Catalina
pretends to be
a unity,
one integrated, darkly well stated,
mysterious silhouette.

—

But the Sun
will have the final sway,
the curtain, now reddening,
where fire streams burn
long and rising
to the South,
broad and sinking
to the North.

—

Let only nightfall
overcome.

—

The clouds are deepening
into something like cerise
which no human artist
could ever mix.

—

The clouds
are sculpted and streaked
by charcoaling
with heavenly felt tips,
and it glows more so.

—

As the island profile darkens more
stars begin to appear there
like blinking beacons
gathering my eye.

—

But, distractingly,
straight ahead of me
to the North
is the point of Laguna Beach
moving from right to left
outlined and filled
with the flickering lights
of Las Brisas
framed by the hard outline
of the winter drooped tall palms
to the left of which
we are still treated
to a gradient from above
of deeper blue
smokily azure limned
fading into pastel grey
faintly smeared with orange
again.

—

Now here on the sea
are the lights
of far off ships
heading out and back
from China
and beyond.

—

night

—

falls.

Carole Luther

Beauregard

I remember you in the sunlight
on the path in my morning garden;
yellow fur and slitted eyes—
full-on predator, you

seeking the mice and rabbits
who had been frolicking the night before
between the rows of lettuce.

While you slept at my feet
even the blue jays were afraid of you then;

sleek and muscular, full of mischief,
sneaking nibbles out of my pies
as they cooled in those summer evenings
on our kitchen windowsill.

You left me presents on the door mat:
a mouse, a bird, even once a possum
never fully eaten. I knew they were
a testament of your devotion

and there was that patch of catnip, remember?

Your ears, marked with notches
from tousles with other neighborhood felines,
lent an air of distinction
to an otherwise plain-old tabby.

In later years you were content
to sleep by the wood stove,
paws pressed against the warmth,
remembering, in dreams, those rabbits chased
down into holes that for me
will never end.

Mary Mackey

Clutter

Sometimes the weight of living
stamps you flat as
a dime

the unread books
& unpaid bills
the dust &
dead people
email, ivy
rotten pipes

stocks that fell
businesses that went bust
languages you forgot
nights spent
staring at the ceiling
beside closets stuffed with
clothes you can no longer
wear

all those love songs you
wrote that never quite
came together
10 with first lines that showed
a promise of seduction
3 with fair middles

then
confusion

verbs with no
subjects

strange
hairs
in your bathroom sink
the ends splayed like
ropes.

Sarah Maclay

Verse

You unfold the morning caviar, peel the wrapper from a pat of butter which I'll smear across croissants. You deliver pearls on a platter. I'll add tiny beads of fish and whirl the string across your teeth. There. Here's a breath of coffee, here's the crescent of my thumbnail drawn across your tongue. Here's the grainy meat of pear, vanilla, coffee beans like berries almost moistening with heat. Fog pads us from the rush of day, the clam's wings slip open, and it's not such a long way from one mouth to another. Nuzzle the morsel inside, examine the surface of the inner shell. That small orange tongue of lox—slip it into your mouth. Insert the butter knife between the pages of 'A Thousand French Verbs.' *Vivre. Vernir. Verser.* To live, to varnish, to decant, to pour, fill, deposit, overturn, to shed, to spill. Take this long strand of rain from my mouth into yours. And wear this strange gray weather like a cloak.

Amy MacLennan

Negotiations With Landlord's Canary

A simple enough transaction:
for you a week at my place,
for me a hundred bucks off the rent.

But it's been three days
and you're not eating.

The Hoover incident I accept
as my fault. In my own defense,
I was late for a date.

But all you've done
is perch on the hutch.

I understand your reserve
after the introduction to Spike,
a poorly formulated plan.

But come for a nibble,
a peck at some apple.

The smoke alarm, a fluke,
won't bother you again.
I bought a new toaster.

But you've got to eat, so please
fly down.
I will offer millet,
jangle keys, give you seed from my hand
and if it makes any difference,

changes anything at all,
I will praise you, admire you,

honor you.

Devorah Major

October Ritual

1.

this year as last the sky
a cloudless azure blue
just like the fifty cent postcard
said it would be   breaking
only when touched by land or sea

the air again smelled of the last
days of summer just a tongue tip
breeze to remind you of
october instead of june

when rumbles cut the afternoon in two
and a shriek of silver gray bombers
stabbed the wind   tore
the soft underbelly of the sky
leaving spiral signatures of icy oil
against the shadow of blue

they proclaim themselves angels
as they trumpet the power of war
but school children who know
the truth of battlefields
cover their ears
crouch under benches
begin to cry

2.

the nurse in labor and delivery
smiles remembering the afternoon
her oldest son ran and spun unable
to be still in the middle of the flag
waving crowd of applause for the
war plane gymnastics

as she told us how the bombers swooped
and swaggered crossed each other broadly
as they looped each loop
she placed her hand across her rounded

midriff and realized that she would not mind
if it held another boy child

3.

as i listen to her story
i see her softly laugh
i notice that her auburn hair is a bit
shorter but just as dark   her olive face fuller
but hands as long as the mother in albania
who has just buried most of her family
and now becomes a newspaper caption
naming her ethnic and poor
and alone

4.

americans seem to be in favor of clean war
enjoy blue angel images in movies
on television, in iraq
in afhghanistan or the sudan

pure wars where our boys
rarely get shot down
and film footage only shows
fireworks against the night's black sky

5.

a cluster of boys have been born
in our row of houses

three abutting homes
three young black women
give birth over four years
to five boys

they say it is a sign of war

Lee Mallory

Standing on Bacon

I like
outdoor cooking:
I cook in cans,
and avoid dishes.
I serve on newspapers.

Today I cooked
slices of Midwest bacon
over Mexican "hotwood."

Then I pressed it
in several sections
of the *LA Times*.

I soaked out strips
between church pedophiles
& death by "friendly fire."

Standing & pressing,
I almost heard
it squeal.

Adrianne Marcus

Les Origines du Langage (Painting, 1955) The Origins of Language

"A Stone Which Does Not Think, Thinks The Absolute" —Rene Magritte

What was the first word like? A grunt, a high pitched keening
Over the body, the first emerging, the other, leaving. Was it even
A word, or simply the body letting air rush to the surface, like
The heart trying not to drown? Then the deep intake, the fresh
Smell of birth, that bloody welcome. Or death, that sour odor the
Body produces like old wax, thick, crepuscular.

Only the stone at the cave's entrance could hear, or perhaps the
Women in attendance who would make cooing noises, like thin
Birds flying in and out of a dark place, trying to navigate by light,
By instinct, their dull grey wings and dun bodies always hungry.
Or perhaps it was rage: all the metallic voices of blood and copper
Bound up in one unearthly scream. That would be the first word.
That would be the last.

Clint Margrave

Blind Leading the Blind

There is a blind man
waiting patiently
at the corner of
this busy intersection.

No stoplight resides here,
so he listens attentively
for the afternoon traffic
to come to a halt.

A young girl on
her way home
from school
has stopped to watch him.

I, too, have slowed down
my car enough to
spy on him through
the rearview mirror.

When the last car passes,
he proceeds without
care or caution, safely
to the other side;

leaving only the girl and I
to gaze blankly upon
an empty crosswalk
with two stunned faces

that he will never see.

SO LUMINOUS THE WILDFLOWERS

Melanie Martin

Class Insecta

He had pinned some alive, slender metal
through flesh. Some I recognized:
house fly, moth, butterfly, beetle—
common names he called them *common people
say them. This is a Black-winged Damselfly.*
Its wings were reddish-black.
And this is a Clubtail Dragonfly,
wings of lace and scales, tube tail with bulged tip.

I liked the *common* beetle, its iridescent shell.
Ground Beetle, he said and pointed with a pencil tip,
See the mandibles, two fangs for chewing,
*beetles chew not suck. Here is the thorax
where legs or wings are and this is the abdomen.*

We lay side-by-side; he touched my abdomen
with fingers that held small bodies, drove pins
straight down their soft middles, *thorax.*
I thought of the killing jars in his basement,
ethyl acetate—one last frightened breath.
When his hand grazed my neck, I flinched.
He said *Have you been choked before?*

Holaday Mason

Inside the Radio

are these steps I take across this street, some
old movie popcorn, four fresh clams, an empty martini
glass, Miles Davis, twelve white Gerber daisies, a twisted
oak tree, a door, a hallway, an unpacked suitcase
and some golden
bamboo. Inside the radio is
the scent of night blooming jasmine in full bloom. Inside the radio
are many sets of dentures, the electrical currents
that make an epileptic seize, a woman's alto lullaby
sung into her baby's open mouth and a once fine Persian rug.
Inside the radio is the conversation between
two Iranian women walking an Israeli beach
and a bird house full of yellow and green canaries. Inside
the radio are the wheels of a small girl's
roller skates and her furry pink bedroom slippers.
Inside the radio is the sound of falling water.
Inside the radio are eight perfect smoke rings.
Inside the radio are all the old Easter rabbits, a stack of wet firewood,
a newspaper headline from May, 14, 1923 and the two hours
you're allowed to park on the right side of the street in front of your house.
Inside the radio are a bunch of plastic bags
for the dog shit of strange dogs. Inside the radio
is a mother's hand in her mother's hand, is the dew
of Irish wool on a pair of knitting needles,
an orange traffic cone, a lower case letter "l"
and one flawless cherry blossom open and wet.
Inside the radio is a pair of sandals.
Inside the radio is the twitch of a tail,
three freshly ironed cotton dresses worn by slave women,
a moving violation for jaywalking,
two gangsters 12 and 11 years old respectively,
guns in their big pants, carbon on their fingers.
Inside the radio is a watch
on a fob spinning around, vagrant drumbeats spinning
through the air, the footsteps of a man
in your past (your father? your brother?), the bones of your face,
a pearl of semen on the tip of a penis and
the way an adolescent girl smells of toast and skin.
Inside the radio is some hot Cuban music.
Inside the radio is the Buddha
and his two dogs, are ten worn out bibles,
and a perfumed soap on a rope.

Inside the radio there are lots of skeletons,
two are in black tie attire. One wears a redressed red dress.
There's the afore mentioned music, a wicked chocolate birthday cake,
and the faces of all your relatives carved into masks
you can show to those who are not yet born.
Inside the radio are two roan horses
(the ones you always wanted),
leather saddles, bridles, stirrups
and the fields, the wild new snow fields
over which to run.

Ryan Masters

Da Vinci Lumbers Through the Sistine Chapel

The abbess lets her sisters test
the secret flying instrument,
and one by one they pedal through
the lofty air of the high room.
She calls instructions out,
soft hands cupped around her mouth.
Beneath the arching painted sky
the machine is flapping up and down
suspended in the atmosphere
by cranks and belts and spinning wheels
as God with his fingers reaches
out to touch its vellum wings.

Ellyn Maybe

I've Got Something Orange to Tell You

I've never gotten a Valentine's Day card in August before.
In fact, I haven't gotten a Valentine's Day card in February
since 1969.
When I found Sheila Castle's 800 cards in her Batman lunch box,
I stole her Valentine from Billy Stevens.
He gave her one with flower bubble gum XXX'd like a courtship.
Billy was cool.
He used to trip me in milk line.
He did cool things.
He never apologized.
He's a stockbroker now.
I'm broke now.
But then I had to steal that card.

I'm an honest girl.
I have to tell you that so this truth has more credibility.
Once I ordered a double cheeseburger
and McDonalds gave me three pieces of meat.
I gave it back.
And to show them how adamant I was, I turned vegetarian.
So there, Billy.

Somewhere Sheila Castle must be thinking to Billy Stevens,
she didn't exist.
Those extra long looks during duck duck goose must have meant
nothing to him cause why didn't he give her a card February 14.
Sheila, baby, I stole it.

I was knock kneed with loneliness.
Nocturnal glasses.
Vultures caught this bookworm.

Oh childhood, you delinquent moment between pampers and bras.

Anyway when I took Billy's card, I scribbled to Ellyn on it
to make my forged career, pre-Alan Rudolph,
the moderns, Keith Carradine,
surreal Matisse, toe shoes complete.

Valentine's Day cards from parents don't count.

Besides, even though I stole Billy's affection in the lunch box,
I left one cream cheese sandwich (with extra butter),
one apple, and one picture of Shakespeare.

Let's say we traded nutrition.
Good! I'll sleep better tonight!!

Terry McCarty

Icarus' Itinerary

Fly high in the sky.
Allow wings to be melted
by the sun.
Fall to Earth.
Suffer painful injuries.
Hire a PR firm to do damage control.
Apologize to Jay, Dave, Conan,
Larry, Connie, Iyanla,
Dr. Phil, Barbara and Oprah.
Confess past sins
to a sympathetic journalist.
Do a photo shoot for
VANITY FAIR.
Get a suspended sentence,
contingent on completing
200 hours of community service.
Go to a rehab center in Malibu.
Become clean and sober.
Get a new pair of wings.
Feel immortal.
Repeat all of the above.

Michael McClintock

Whales at Santa Cruz

This place she loved above all others on the coast,
at this same time of year, the fall.
We came each year to watch the whales.
She was small and from the gulls she had learned
how to lean forward and balance herself
against the blast of wind.

She was propped on pillows and sitting up in bed
when with that same motion she leaned forward and died.

I have waited for darkness; it is illegal to release
human remains here.
I am told three hundred whales will pass this rock point tonight.
As they pass, they will sing.

I have heard before the voices of these creatures, on recordings;
I have sampled their grammar and measured the entropy of their phrasing:
the clicks and squeals, the unpredictable trilling, the small chirps
like those in a twilit garden at the borders of hearing.
I have come to a few conclusions about those songs,
their theme and sequence, but they are improbable conclusions.

The wind is light and fills all the space above the sea
like a giant's sleeping breath. The kelp forest stirs.

Her ashes—
a moment's haze
then clear ocean.

Jeffrey McDaniel

The Benjamin Franklin of Monogamy

Reminiscing in the drizzle of Portland, I notice the ring
that's landed on your finger, a massive insect

of glitter, a chandelier shining at the end of a long tunnel.
Thirteen years ago, you hid the hurt under the blanket

of your voice, said *I guess there's two kinds of women.
Those you write poems about, and those you don't.*

It's true. I never slid sonnets under the door, or served you
haiku in bed. My idea of courtship was tapping

Jane's Addiction lyrics in Morse code on your window
at three hundred a.m., whisky doing push-ups

on my breath. I worked within the confines of my character,
cast as the bad boy in your life, the Magellan

of your dark side. We don't have a past so much as a bunch
of electricity, power never put to good use. *What*

we had together makes it sound like a virus, as if
we caught one another like a flu, and desire was merely

a symptom that could be treated with soup and lots of sex.
Gliding beside you now, I feel like the Ben Franklin

of monogamy, as if I invented it, but I'm still not immune
to your waterfall scent, haven't developed antibodies

for your smile. I don't know long *regret* existed
before humans hammered a word on it, or how many

paper towels it would take to wipe up the Pacific Ocean,
or why the light of a candle being blown out

travels faster than the luminescence of one that's freshly lit,
but I do know all our huffing and puffing

into the other's throat—as if the heart was a birthday cake
covered with trick candles—didn't make the silence

any easier to navigate. I'm sorry all the kisses I scribbled
on your neck were written in disappearing ink, sorry

this poem took thirteen years to reach you. Sometimes
I thought of you so hard one of your legs would pop out

of my ear, and when I slept, you'd press your face
against the porthole of my submarine. I wish that just once,

instead of joyriding over flesh, we'd put our hands away
like chocolate to be saved for later, and deciphered

the calligraphy of each other's eyelashes, translated
a paragraph from the volumes of what couldn't be said.

The First Straw
for Christine Caballero

I used to think love was two people sucking
on the same straw to see whose thirst was stronger,

but then I whiffed the crushed walnuts of your nape,
traced jackals in the snow-covered tombstones of your teeth.

I used to think love was a non-stop saxophone solo
in the lungs, till I hung with you like a pair of sneakers

from a phone line, and you promised to always smell
the *rose* in my kerosene. I used to think love was terminal

pelvic ballet, till you let me jog beside while you pedaled
all over hell on the menstrual bicycle, your tongue

ripping through my prairie like a tornado of paper cuts.
I used to think love was an old man smashing a mirror

over his knee, till you helped me carry the barbell
of my spirit back up the stairs after my car pirouetted

in the desert. You are my history book. I used to not believe
in fairy tales till I played the dunce in sheep's clothing

and felt how perfectly your foot fit in the glass slipper
of my ass. But then duty wrapped its phone cord

around my ankle and yanked me across the continent.
And now there are three thousand miles between the *u*

and *s* in esophagus. And being without you is like standing
at a cement-filled well with a roll of Yugoslavian nickels

and making a wish. Some days I miss you so much
I'd jump off the roof of your office building

just to catch a glimpse of you on the way down. I wish
we could trade left eyeballs, so we could always see

what the other sees. But you're here, I'm there,
and we have only words, a nightly phone call—one chance

to mix feelings into syllables, to pour into the receiver,

hope they don't disassemble in that calculus of wire.

And lately—with this whole war thing—the language machine
supporting it—I feel betrayed by the alphabet, like they're

injecting strychnine into my vowels, infecting my consonants,
naming attack helicopters after shattered Indian tribes:

Apache, Blackhawk; and West Bank colonizers are settlers,
so Sharon is Davey Crockett, and Arafat: Geronimo,

and it's the Wild West all over again. And I imagine Picasso
looking in a mirror, decorating his face in war paint,

washing his brushes in venom. And I think of Jenin
in all that rubble, and I feel like a Cyclops with two eyes,

like an anorexic with three mouths, like a scuba diver
in quicksand, like a shark with plastic vampire teeth,

like I'm the executioner's fingernail, trying to reason
with the hand. And I don't know how to speak love

when the heart is a busted cup filling with spit and paste,
and the only sexual fantasy I have is busting

into the Pentagon with a bazooka-sized pen and blowing
open the minds of generals. And I comfort myself

with the thought that we'll name our first child Jenin,
and her middle name will be Terezin, and we'll teach her

how to glow in the dark, and how to swallow firecrackers,
and to never neglect the first straw, because no one

ever talks about the first straw, it's always the last straw
that gets all the attention, but by then it's way too late.

Daniel McGinn

inkblot

rub my cheek i am new
less mineral more cloud
puffed like an éclair

saint augustine
stayed green in the summer
required little attention but made the skin itch
stick-man arms in pink patch patterns

i used to climb from the crib to the top of the dresser
to turn on the radio
i could hear little richard singing even when the radio was turned off

i had a patio a back porch a red picnic table a black dog
a pink brick fence red hibiscus a power mower and a big
green rake

i couldn't tell you what was said before no
meant no
this was before pain had first names
this was milk on demand warm skin and sleep
plenty of sleep

construction paper walls
the trees outside were bare
the sand box sand is gray and wet
i know my colors
no is no

here i am in the child's chair
how many fingers? i have teeth
i brush them in the morning
the sink is taller today.
how many channels?
kellogg's. quick draw mcgraw.
mine. these are my toys.
my mom. my lawn. my house.
we don't hit girls

my hand is round and stubby worms
nails clear like wet shells
pony hair is stiff and smells and dirt

feels better than a dog

this is the part where i fall like snow
my arms have gone to heaven
you kissed me on the bus
beyond the windows the world was white

there were oranges and smudge pots in winter morning
stomp my feet between the cracks
stomp on lucky strike pack
between the trees my breath was fog
i pretend i am smoking

do you remember your fist in my face?
i do

your eyes were cold as marbles
the blood on your shirt was mine
you were jealous of everything

my knees were green from saint augustine
rain fell in my eyes
dry leaves and twigs grew out of my hair

Lori McGinn

Untitled

Although the black rose
in the vase on my table
is just a symbol,
death is as real as
the red blood on my palette.

I don't want to go to bed;
it is too close to being normal.
I'm lying here,
flushed cheek to the cold tile floor,
still listening for the blackberry killers.

June Melby

Animals?

Truthfully, my favorite wild animals in the world would have to be my toes, you know, the small ones especially, they are out of control! You don't want to turn your back when they're around—*nosiree*—they will sneak up on you and steal your nuts, scatter your berries, I'm not kidding, I don't kid around like I used to!

Once while wearing a pair of open-toed sandals, (cork sole), my left big toe was found organizing a protest, painting picket signs: "More days at the beach", "I hate socks" and "Down with coffee tables."

Encourage hobbies such as "coin-on-the-floor-picking-upping" and "try-to-grab-the-remote-control-no-hands." It is the best way to keep your *toesies* in line, and therefore, happy. Ice cream, recommended, don't skimp on birthdays.

Say your prayers each night, my friends. Give thanks for your toes, but pray they stay right down on your feet where they are, never discovering a way to leap off and crawl around town, poking their little toe-y heads around street corners, startling the children.

Carol Moldaw

Stanford Hills

Tiptoe on a sturdy branch,
taller than the tallest girl,
she reaches into the sky

and pulls at a tangled thread.
Rows of clouds unpurl.
She can see miles ahead,

she can almost see Webb Ranch
across the tawny hills,
its silos, horse barns, fields,

and the two rickety shacks
where they buy vegetables
from Mexican women whose men

bending over harvest fields
fill giant burlap sacks.
She'd like to have a sack

to wear for Halloween.
She'd sew beads on the hem
and be an Indian maiden.

Bright feathers down her back!
Last year, as Fairy Queen
in a tinsel diadem,

she waved her foil wand
and charmed the cul-de-sac.
Now she jumps, rolling beyond

cow flops, ants, a scraped shin;
flattened fields of rye;
her mother calling her in.

Jim Natal

Chopping Onions With my Sister

Chilly, as L.A. Thanksgivings go, a cream
of wheat and oatmeal in a tom-tom box
kind of morning. But we are focused on tonight,
and a table laid with heirloom china, a golden bird.
I am trying a new stuffing recipe, always risky
because family expects the familiar, the firm,
layered roundness of tradition. My youngest sister
stands beside me at the counter, respective choices
of knives in our hands. There are onions
to be chopped, kitchen tears to be avoided. She says
keeping the onions cold does the trick,
or to peel them at the sink; cool running water
is the secret. I prefer the technique of not speaking;
a closed mouth is supposed to foil the fumes.
It sort of works, but by the fourth onion the tingling
begins, then a smoldering in my nostrils
that flares to my eyes and the well caps burst.

My sister, whose tear ducts always have malfunctioned,
tells me of her new job and her disappointment with it.
How this year her goal is to finally learn to drive.
And, of course, that brings up our mother, whom
she hasn't seen in a couple of years—mom's feelings
of being trapped in the home since she had to
let her car go and license expire. Her continued denials
that a hearing aid, so expensive, will be of any help.

My sister has grown quiet. She sighs and tells me
we have to talk, that she wants to unburden a weight
she's dragged for years. She feels I wasn't
there for her when she needed me most,
that telephone calls and my close monitoring
from a coastal distance were not enough.
She doesn't want to hear my reasons
again: job strain, debris of collapsed marriage,
taking care of mom and my daughter, her only niece.
She's past it now, my sister says.
She forgives me, she says and wants to just go on.
My jaw clenches, riled tongue subdued
against back of teeth. As if dozens more onions
have suddenly tumbled onto the cutting board,

need urgent slicing, I press my lips together tight.
Because there's a turkey to get in the oven.
Because of sweet potatoes and tart cranberries.
Because Tania and Jade are beginning to set the table
and mom and Barbara will be here any minute.

Gwynn O'Gara

From a Clear Height

Even a dying gladiola
looks beautiful as it stretches
into sunlight on the deck.

The rosemary bush needs pruning.
Those downward thrusts feel sad,
an old man's beard someone's neglected to trim.

Whitecaps all day on the bay.
In the clean air everything looks as if
it belongs right where it is.

Beyond our deck, beyond the office towers
and beyond the golden hill of Bernal
is the mountain my mother lies buried behind.

Today, a sunny day enjoyed inside,
I see it for the first time.
The least of you is not far away at all.

And although you are not here,
you are everywhere: in my son's eyes,
my ears, our grateful pulse, the clouds.

Jamie O'Halloran

Knock Wood

I'll tell you the problem with the probated
Walls of this house—the persistent nicotine
Weeping behind the glaze and paper, the new
Extravagant plaster—is the man who died
Here. Nothing to do but tear out the walls,
Ceiling and floor for the stench of all
His years soaked into that back room.

Today I learn a friend is gone at 33. I don't have
To ask what took him, but recall how the last time
We met we swapped stories with superstitious
Wonder at who still thrived. This house is filled
With elegy: white cat, his paintings, the tiniest
Mexican skull. What is living but elegy?
These old houses we rent to make our own.

David Olivera

Prologue to a Sad Spring

The sun rose to small clouds
marring a perfect ascent.
The cold rain of morning
abandoned the sky to a thin yellow light
that cast uncertainty
into the shape of an elm
across the barn's aging wall.
This was the first day her shovel
would rest against the backyard fence,
the last day she would consider weather
in the plan for tomatoes in her garden.
Already her eyes had grown
into the color of the first memory
that betrayed her.
If wisdom is love for the world
despite what we know, she was wise—
though she did not notice those signs,
so obvious now,
portending the great sadness to come.
Her attention was turned toward
a mockingbird ending breakfast with a song,
and to the bright pink in the bud of a plum tree
ready to flower, to the scent of water
slipping from blades of grass into
the growing dirt, and to
the small words she picked from sunlight
to remind herself later
of so much happiness.

Judith Pacht

Recipe for S&M Marmalade

Blood oranges
should be eaten
naked,
blushing,
cupped
in the palm.
Easily entered,
fingers
separate skin from flesh,
carefully pulling
segment by segment,
opening the ruby-orange,
rosy-wet.

Ignore
the rest:
the bitter Sevilles,
Hamlins
the under-ripe
green-tinged,
the rusty orange.
Mottled.
Rough.
Sour.

Leave them
to the flash
of a newly whetted blade
sharp and cold
cutting into skin and flesh.
Slice.
Soak.
Turn up heat.
Boil until flesh melts
and bubbles blister
thick deep orange.

Think only of the end,
the mouth-feel,
the stew of dark sweet
and juice
and thickened pulp

to swallow.

Jaimes Palacio

Dialogue

The small fishing boat rocks in the middle
of the Pacific reciting iambic-pentameter
in Portuguese.

At the base camp on Mount Everest, the air
thinning the higher you go, the wind carries
the remnants of Haiku.

In Antarctica even the ice quotes Anais Nin.

From Belgrade to Tokyo.
Jakarta to New York.
Santa Monica to the Space Station.

Town and City.
Ghetto and Suite.

Ringing in the Ides with the crucible
of an endangered art, lost children
reclaim their birthrights, celebrating the same
tongue (no matter the language.)

For this trembling pause we are all of the same
color.

We are all of the same music.

There are no borders.

Or traffic.

Or federal agendas.

How delicate this moment is.

How tender our hands raised
towards the sun.

Robert Peters

Cousin Albert

He hoed the corn, split wood, and
curried the horses. His stepdad
often beat the bastard with horse
harness and a whip. When he'd
return from swimming, he got
another vicious trimming.
He smiled at strangers, excelled at
school, was lithe with jet black
eyes and hair. One stormy night I
slept with him, my boy-foot snug
inside his underwear.

He bought a Model-T, gabardine
pants, a white shirt and a tie from
his job in Holperin's grocery store.
He'd marry Francine Kalous and
move to Alaska. That spring when
he begged off ploughing, half-
brother James attacked him with
an axe. His leg was hacked. Aunt
Kate, his Mom broke a board over
his back. He ran to Minnow lake,
dove to the bottom, retrieved muck.

Holly Prado

Harry, It's Raining

Your knees against mine as we sleep. 5 A.M. —
ah, there's time, still, to stay here in bed.

When I do get up,

I sit at my desk in my pajamas with two candles lit
and Tibetan peace incense burning. My payer lifts
with the lively twists of smoke:

May the day pass smoothly so we can get to evening
when we plan to eat out, then see a movie, then come home
and go to sleep again. What an ordinary prayer, I hope
not an insult to the Tibetan Buddhists who made the incense,

who built a floor-to-ceiling mandala for Universal Peace, all
by hand, infusing it with everything they, enlightened monks,
understand about peace for the entire world. But isn't
creating peace

in one's own life a step toward the whole? Aren't our knees,
gently touching, a mandala forming peaceful symmetry?
Maybe tonight we're doing our best for peace when we eat
at Zumaya's, then settle in to watch an Italian movie about
the Mafia. Kurt Vonnegut once wrote that if there are angels,
he wants them organized along the lines of the Mafia. I agree.
Tightly-knit bands of angels could surely do more good than
flittery, independent-contractor angels. As the incense
smoke curls, I believe in angels; in Buddhism's intricate cosmos;

in Catholic saints; in our plain, Protestant carpenter—
Christ. He said "Love." That's it. That's my prayer,
breathed into the sweet-smelling incense. Love. Peace.
Nothing new, but so what? The day opens itself as I pray for

our knees, my darling, which touch each other with the
delicacy of folded angel wings. We are saving the world
with our knees. Knees for peace.

R.A.C.

Grace

We live on the second floor of a motel
facing the 22 onramp, in a town so hip,
even the Mormon missionaries rock pompadours
and Razor scooters.

Every night we are kept away from our dreams
by the constant noise of someone else's going
and tires screeching like hysterical women—
my daughter watches this from the window.

I look into her eyes,
see a whirl of traffic collecting behind them.

She is no longer fascinated by how the television
and lamps are bolted to the dresser, or the little
bars of soap resembling Hershey's miniatures.

Our neighbors change weekly.
She doesn't ask if their children can come over to play
anymore.

> Microwave dinners and ice buckets,
> drippy condoms hung to dry on the balcony railing,
> that creepy kid in 133 with cataracts,
> strollers being used as shopping carts,
> sixteen-year old couples paying a night's rate
> with their lunch money,
> the Echo Park reject tossing H to his customers
> through the hole in his screen,
> an Indian man constantly winking and asking our names,
> and a soda machine that actually sells cherry Pepsi.

At least three nights a week we eat cereal for dinner.
The crib doubles as a laundry basket.
Nobody stops by just to say, "hi."
Yesterday Piper asked if Santa would know
where to find us.

Right now, someone from my home town is wondering
if I ever made it to Hollywood.

The television is broken, stuck

on a station reporting the same child, missing,
only this time, wearing a different body.

Today, blond hair, brown eyes, 73 lbs.
Tomorrow, brown hair, brown eyes, 77 lbs.

She asks me, "Mommy, why?"
I tell her I don't know.

I've yet to figure out the difference
between scaring the shit out of her and keeping her
informed, so we watch the broken television that costs
$1200 a month,

the television that will remain
bolted to the dresser long after we are gone

because sometimes
people take things

that don't belong to them.

Raindog

Tank Farm

Lou was welding
on top of the tank
when a spark ignited
a ghost vapor
and blew him
clean in half.
I couldn't stop
shakin' for a week
so the company sent
me to Port Angeles.
Beneath the Olympic
Glaciers I finally
slept easy and
the coffee began to
taste good again.

Soutine's Palette

Encased in a plexi-glass display
at the LA County Museum of Art
is the last palette of the painter
Chiam Soutine:
two boards held
together by hinges so
encrusted with paint
that no trace of rust
decays their purpose.
The palette is a deep green
as if by some foundation of color
the painter Soutine might
create his lively portraiture
and fluid landscapes.
The palette is bordered on
two sides with fat globs of
paint: little mountains of muted
browns, reds, blues and yellows
that rise above that flattened
plain of green, colors that appear
dulled by stillness, unused
for nearly fifty five years.
We see the palette as *artifact*
with its border of knobby
paint waiting patiently for
Soutine's returning hand and
stabbing brush to awaken
the life that lays dormant
within the skin of its
mummified pigment,
waiting for his next
inspiration to summon
forth the magic of color
and light.

Robert Roden

California Dreaming

This city is plump with extravagance—
But on the streets below, some
Collect bottles and pillows.

Glass rattles through the night
As if the charming wind struck chimes
Instead of coursing through the bones

Of men and women. I hear sirens
Eleven floors below me, but in a trendy
Restaurant we drink Mai-Tais and listen

To heated conversations rising on
A current of upwardly mobile thoughts.
This is where we ascend, we aspire.

John C. Rodriguez

Halloween Curse

"And who are you supposed to be?"
asks the lady in the nice house.

Dumbstruck, I stare.

She's a witch
and indirectly shakes a bone-gnarled,
green, thin-skinned finger.
Chin and nose forms like
stalagmite and stalactite.
(Maybe they'll meet in another 1000 years!)

Her eyes are the velvet blue haze around the full moon.
Matted gray hair.
Toad warts throb.

Specious smiling maw is guarded
by a handful of flesh-stained teeth.

Her familiar,
a black cat named Never,
slow brushes against her ankle boots.

She offers her cauldron of festering candy corn
and I forget the question
until now,

25 years later.

Danny Romero

Dreams

In a dream I ask my father
if he had ever been to Chicago.
"No," he answered, adding
that he saw more of the world
than he wanted as a 1st division
marine in the South Pacific
during World War Two: Okinawa,
Iwo Jima and Guadalcanal.
Afterwards, the idea was to
stay close to home: California,
Los Angeles and Watts.

And my mother liked it
too, he said,
in a conversation longer
than any we had
when he was alive.

Lee Rossi

John the Apostle

I did not know who spoke to me
        at the end of a night
                filled with dreams of death and war

but I saw men
        rising into the sky
                whose tears were bombs

They had the look of those
        who had died many times
                and yet each day rose again

ready for another death
        The sockets where their eyes had been
                were filled with birds

sweet green singers
        and flowers
                with many seeds

They did not look like men
        but like bales of barbed wire
                left to rot in a field

Their feet were formed of rust
        and crumbled the instant
                they touched the earth

They showed me all the beauty
        of killing, blood flowers
                blooming on my own pale body

and then He came to me
        the Prince of Snow
                Digger of Channels

He kissed my wounds
        drinking from each of them
                till I was transparent

as a sheet of ice
        my heart and lungs
                swimming beneath the surface

Tell them this, He said
        but I turned away and ran
                as if I had seen my own Death

and still I heard Him
        calling, *There is no Pain*
                I have not suffered

I am the Voice
        of Stone singing
                the Avalanche

I am the Wave made
        by Everything that Falls
                I pass through Skin like Thought

and, yes, I could feel Him
        moving inside me now
                as if I were about to give birth

and though I am only a man
        I would have opened myself
                from groin to heart

to give Him entry
        the Child of every Mother
                into the world

Jim Rue

Ancestry

I sat naked on the bank of the frigid Missouri River.
I peeked down from my tenth floor window on Kansas City.
I went to bed and I dreamed I explored this town where my parents were married in 1930.
No Missouri plaque marks my first glimmer of legitimacy.
But Bonnie and Clyde did the town once.
Ma Barker and Alvin Karpis stayed in this very place.
Jesse James has streets named after him.
But no entree is named after my mother at the Savoy Hotel.
No musical style is attributed to my father in suburban Shawnee Mission.
Bob Dole never knew my father. Jamie Farr has never heard my name.

Still, those incendiary two, Opal and Arthur,
Left a light deep in the eyes of their progeny.
Anguished depression refugees begat
Anguished language people like me.
Mom couldn't help telling her story.
Over Scrabble, with pizza, during the movie, any time.
She cried but never knew how.
She took things, but never knew what.
My father, Ozark coal-miner's son, was a hulking, deaf orphan of the Brethren.
Sin hung from him like Spanish moss.
Was it diphtheria, or the yard bosses' truncheon that killed his hearing?
It was suicide.
His ears refused to hear his children whine, his wife harp.
'Tempest fugits,' he would advise.
It sure does. One of four siblings down.
Two pounding their foreheads now, demanding health.
One limping forward alone, fist in the sky,
Dreaming weakly of five acres and independence
Just as he did.

In my Kansas City dreams my toy doorstop survived the decades.
It was a two by twelve inch wooden drive-in theater
Featured a wooden Saturday matinee idol drawn by me
In pencil. The cowboy with his horse
Was special. Even his horse knew what.
I never knew what, and still don't.
And he listened. His eyes glistened like nailheads.
He talked through his teeth. He smoked, so cool then.
He took the bags of gold and it was "Now, Vamoose!"
He spoke bastard Spanish and brandished a pistola.
J. Edgar Hoover hated his guts.
Kansas was in his cold smile.

Dixie Salazar

Jesus Loves You at the Venue Beauty Salon—Fifth Avenue, Fresno

If the kid is there
I'll tap my gritty quarters
on the glass display
of pink crullers
and tiny, frosted inner tubes
lined up at Jimmy's doughnuts.
He'll pass me his day old
smile, a maple bar, and overlook
the quarters once again.

Jesus Loves You,
but he just puts up with me
I'll sing out the door, passing
the *Sorry, We're Closed* sign
of Open Door Ministries,
my face bobbing over flocks
of red, white and blue angels
and choirs of geishas at Shooting
Star Gifts, on my way
to Venue Beauty Salon
where I empty trash and sweep
up tumbleweeds of hair.
I was married once
to a doctor who gave himself shots
and drank his own pee
didn't last though, maybe
he wasn't a doctor...
Fogged in short wave, the second one
muttered in the cellar all night
with the door closed, big
plans he had to warn the Pentagon—
magnetic storms and secret codes
he broke, with the others like him.
Then there was Fred, big
on curly fries and short
on romance, born again
to Bowling For Jesus...
Found the Lord myself a few times
Venus says, but kept misplacing him...
She pats her brown #5 waves
smooth as one of Jimmy's French twists
and winks out the jingly, abierto door.

In Dumpster Land, whiskey sour blonde
tumbles with mushroom pearl. Brunette
Serenade rolls into unholy
alliance with Jimmy's greasy doilies,
smudged tithing pledges and rusty
hangers from Fifth Avenue—
one giant stripmall hairball.
Hefting a King Cobra from A-1 Liquor
Jimmy toasts the rows of security doors—
business is picking up he says
offering Flaming Hot Cheetos
with a quick bump bump in his eyes.
I want to say that my guy has a big
rig or that I am taken, married
to a cloud in a ceremony attended
only by two sparrows and a broom;
I was given away by the sun, and my wild,
cirrus lover does not clean toenails
with a steak knife, takes me
duro y slow and does not spit
in parking lots. But instead, I say
Gracias, no, slide around the corner
past the balloon bouquets and Jesus
crucified on a palm tree shadowed
by the #28 bus, a blurry alter
of clouds and marked down Marys.
Please God, abierto, abierto—
help the kid get through
the next round of treatments—let Venus
roll her horoscope into one more month
of quarters, abierto, no appointment necessary—
as for me, no shooting stars, I can get by—
just a window of sultry clouds at night,
abierto, so they can slide over the sill
into my room, one small sign of grace
por favor, the opposite of a miracle.

Jim Sandford

The Collector

I kept honey bees in jars and tossed flies
in webs of hedge spiders to watch
them feed, knocked lightening bugs from air
to make sun rings of their luciferin,
held butterflies to feel wing velvet spatter
my fingers the way I won love from girls
to hold their haughty power in my hands.
I teased cats, let fish rot on stream banks,
crushed a land turtle to see if it
had insides and felt its death in my own
but never gave thought to cruelty before
I shot a sparrow
and believed I killed it. I liked birds enough
to dream of flying like one and the still form
made me sad until my penknife popped
the BB from a beak nostril and the bird woke.
When it flew from my hand I stopped
killing and collecting creatures because now
they stared back though holes in life.

Cathie Sandstrom Smith

Ashes, Ashes

I lifted the lid of the square bronze urn, rubbed
the greasy ash between thumb and fingers,
felt my father's remains to make his loss
tangible.

Over Manhattan a fine gray powder:
acres of ash, pulverized concrete, cables—
tumbled sinews thick as a man's wrist,
fine threads of radial tires sprung
like piano wire, hideous cacophony.
Currents of smoke drift through honeycombed
sheets of teetering steel. Errant leaves
of paper lift in the interrupted air.

A thousand thousand images later
I am still waiting for this truth to be real.

Send me then, a vial of ash.
Something of the acrid wind
I can take into myself. Something
I can touch.

Barton M. Saunders

The Waiting

A caterpillar circles
on the bottom step
of my stairwell

I place leaves
in his pathway

as a gentle suggestion
that tiered existence
is dangerous,

but the leaves go
missing in the night,

and he remains
evolving in revolutions
of solitude and order

Sharon Saunders

Winter

This time of year
Days shorten into ever
Widening bands of darkness
The sun travels across the sky
Low and stealthily
Dragging shadows into long
Slithering ghosts
Disappearing into the night

The squirrel
With its layer of
The fat of many acorns
Finds a safe and still
Corner underground
To sleep the long sleep of winter

Biding their time with others
Of their flock
Snowbirds fly to
The sunny barren
Lands far to the South
To await the Northern Spring

I miss the sounds of the children
The medley of bird songs
That arises with the dawn
I gather memories
Around me as a warm woolen shawl
Woven in the many colors
Of my life

Larry Schulz

Marriage Versus Trout Fishing

You have to remember
The squirming worm
Is taken from
Its safe Styrofoam mud home
And painfully pinned
On curved steel
Until soaked off
Or until death do part.

If it is lucky,
It will end up
In the digestive system
Of another species,
Or it will fall off the hook
After being baited
By a clumsy fingered fisherman
Who groped through the dirt
To find it,
Then held it up
To the morning light
And said,
"This is the one that will do it for me!"

I thought about this
The day you said,
"You are definitely a good catch!"
And looked at me
With a trophy/feed-me glance
As I felt
The air I breathed
Turn to
Water.

Patricia L. Scruggs

The Woman in the Next Car

Rubs her forehead
and I count five gold bracelets.
Then she lays her head
against the headrest
while she waits
for the light to change.

She's somewhere
in her early forties,
going home from work,
with a headache.
Not on her way
to dinner and a show.

Just tired on a Thursday night.
Wishing for—I don't know—
Prince Charming, maybe,
or something more practical
like help with the bills.

Or that her teenage daughter
would open her mouth
and say something pleasant
for a change—talk to her,
that's all,
just talk to her.

Peter Serchuk

Desert Sunrise

Behind me, California sleeps;
the toast barely up in Albuquerque,
the coffee lukewarm in Omaha,
Detroit already revealed for
everything it will never be.
But here, snakes and scorpions
glory in the waking of uncivilized
streets, saguaros stand against
logic and history repeats
its riddle of raucous silence.
A black widow combs her web,
the elf owl sleeps with one eye open,
Harris hawks and diamondbacks
play chess with careless mice...
none of them guessing at love,
none measuring forgiveness,
not one single creature raging
at heaven for a life incomplete
or a home by the sea.

Stephen Shepherd

pharmacon

slovak toast burnt, buttered
with cloves of garlic

chamomile tea with lemon pulp
and spoonful of honey

he clatters in the kitchen
and clangs like some witch

crashing thru the careful,
hidden art of healing

and sick i lie in my bed
wrapped in sheets and sweat

a willing prisoner
well-fed, well-rested

but unable to cleave myself
from the stink and burn of sickness

and unable to heal myself
of the pulp and crush of love

Anne Silver

Shvitzing

Sweat lodges can be scary.
Take this one in Beverly Hills
as we gals climb
into that pill box hat of a hut.
The tent flap covers the opening,
and it gets as dark as a black cashmere cape.
Then the coals are catered to the fire
on antlers and it gets hot so hot
the ice in our diet Cokes melts as quick as alimony.
A few of us scream, and Harold,
our rent-a-Navajo medicine man
scolds us, says we're like *Pablo's* dog—
salivating for comfort.
Then he chants a song,
tells us to confess our sins
against mother nature.
One by one we cry:
Kashish from Tarzana sobs
about abusing the earth
and vows to xeroscape come spring.
Shirley from the Oaks of Sherman weeps,
but then she's been weeping for days.
I think her face lift went fine.
I admit to using my garbage disposal
instead of composting.
The circle of sin complete
the tent flap lifts
and I hunger for something cool.
I look to the west,
watch the winter sun
through the smog—
a scoop of orange gelato
going splat on the blue plate of the Pacific.
The sky goes espresso.

John Oliver Simon

All Over The Place
　　　　for Donald Schenker

Don says *there's poems all over the place,*
it's practically embarrassing, and I nod
without enthusiasm, driving into downtown
Oakland thinking yeah, those two pigeons
squatting on the blue-gray sign HOTEL MORO,
how the part of it that's a poem could fall out
between the word and the bird, or the word *Moro*
all the way back to the reconquest of Spain
and all the bloody hemisphere ending up
on this block I don't care if I see again.

Don says he could just stop anyone
and look at them, they're all so deep
and beautiful, and I say what's interesting
is the stories they all carry around
stranger than fiction, stronger than truth
all these gente waiting to cross the street
each one forgetting their great-grandparents
each one forgetting to tell their children
and I'm no novelist, I can't move a
character across the room, much less two guys
to lunch at a Vietnamese place on Webster.

Over bowls of translucent noodles and odd meat
Don says he always felt like the other poets
were the big boys, and I see how the grand
famous names of his peers, now pushing sixty
have turned into the padded artifacts
of their own careers, while Don's obscurity
has kept him fresh and sweet, and Don says
he loves his tumors, the big one that hurts
in his left hip, the one that's hammering out
among sparse hairs inside his baseball cap,
and though it's his own death that gives him truth
I'm stuck in my heart without any words
while poems in Vietnamese are fluttering up
from all the restaurant tables around us
and escaping into so much empty light.

Maurya Simon

Early Spring

March is a dangerous month.
For two weeks it's all tooth and tirade;
for two more, it's tongue-tied like a girl
worshipping her mirror with moistened lips.

Flesh and reflex wrestle daily
at its frozen altar, davening to sunlight,
that harbinger of winter's undulant undoing.

Green thumbs hitchhike upwards
out of benumbed soil, and the goodly flies
rouse themselves to a fluorescent buzzing.
You see, there's no such thing

as a peaceful revolution—
just watch how pandemonium breaks out
among the waking hormones, how clouds line up

to flex their biceps, how the maples
swoon like mermaids swept ashore half-naked.
Every being is tantalized with being
and feels immortal.

March is more dangerous
than the sirens' call, its mouth gaping,
its hoary heart timing itself to yours,

its petticoats of ice melting,
its white blouse slowly unbuttoning itself,
its breath growing hotter and more uneven—
its touch the tenderest of moments.

Willie Sims

Christine Ambrose

He came that Spring to live with her.
She had written letters.
Just to him.
She was the first woman to call him a man.
Her man she said.
She swore she would always be there for him.
And when he came that first time, she was waiting.
Just for him.
Sitting properly prim on her front porch.
In her favorite soft blue dress with lace collar, and neat black shoes.
Her hair pulled back in a bun.
She flirted with her dancing dark eyes.
And he gloried in her smell of hot buttered truth and thick juicy laughter.
Unlike the comely, caring women who he knew adored him.
Unlike the strong, stately women who he sometimes let hold him.
Unlike the delicate, discreet women who always forgave him.
That first time, instead of offering him her lips,
she had offered her soft hands.
Just like a dear old friend.
And wherever they went,
the long walks on their farm, shopping in town,
they were always like that.
Always holding hands.
Townsfolk would wink to him, smile knowingly,
and tease good naturedly that she had lost her heart,
and was letting him have his way with her.
For together they were shameless.
At night, he would help brush her long hair before they went to bed.
He loved to lay beside her in her huge bed,
smell her good smell, and watch her sleep.
Sometimes, when he thought she had slept long enough,
he would touch her softly, shake her gently, and wake her.
Or if he was tired,
he would simply lie close and still
next to her softness, and sleep too.
And always when she awoke,
she would embrace him, and be there, and say that he was her man.

Those were his cherished memories of her.
Her soft hands. Her soft hair. Her soft heart.
And her good soft smell.
Which is why he now sat crying so hard.

Great shuddering sobs.
While sitting on his father's strong, hard knees.
On these hard, old benches. In this old, big church.
He wanted her softness now.
He desperately wanted to touch her.
He saw her lying there.
And he twisted. And he fretted. And he whined.
And he tried to climb down from his father's hard knees,
and run forward and touch her softness.
"GRANDMAMA! GRANDMAMA!" he wailed.
But they stopped him.
His mother and father shushed him,
and told him that his beloved grandmama had gone "away."
And the preacher in this big, old, church with hickory hard benches
kept repeating that soft, gentle grandmama was "away."
But they all lied. They were all wrong.
He could see her. She was lying right there.
In her favorite soft blue dress.
Just resting, sleeping peacefully like she sometimes did.
He tried to tell them, but they wouldn't listen.
They didn't understand.
If they would just let him go to his grandmama.
And touch her softly. And shake her gently.
And wrap himself in her good grandmama smell, she would awaken.
And her dancing dark eyes would quiet his sobs.
She would hold him to her full soft bosom.
And then, as always, she would call him her "little" man.
If they would just let him go to his grandmama.
And touch her softly. And shake her gently.
He would show them. They would see.
His grandmama was not "away."
She was right there. Just for him.
Just like always.

Joan Jobe Smith

George Harrison

Although I scoffed at Beatlemania in 1964,
thought the 4 long-haired lads ludicrous,
off-key and not fab at all, plus I was in
the throes of morning sickness, pregnant
with my 3ʳᵈ child and when I heard them
screech "I Wanna Hold Your Hand" I got
queasy and always would, despite all that
when the girls in the office played the game
Name Your Favorite Beatle I was a good
sport and picked George for lack of some-
thing better the way I'd've picked eeny
instead of minie or moe. Those bad-boyish
Beatles composed the background music du
jour for the Nowhere men of my generation,
gave them raison d'etre to stop growing up,
get a job, haircuts, go to war, get married.
Mop-topped Peter Pans day tripping with
Eleanor Rigby, garage bands and jabberwocky,
they let it be, did it in the road in yellow sub-
marines, nothing to get hung about while I
was the walrus, Lady Madonna so tired ob-la-
di 8 days a week helter skelter back in the USSR
HELP! rearing 3 kids in strawberry fields that
seemed forever all those decades when not
one time did I have time to think about my
Favorite Beatle George or that I had one until
last week when George died and suddenly I
realized what a hangdog dowdy I'd been and
how that New Years Eve night I'd watched my
no-good hippie husband dancing in the dark
at the party with the pretty airline stewardess
to George Harrison's "Something" and then
take her outside in the moonlight where they
kissed on the lips, George was standing there
in the shadows of the starry night only waiting
for this moment to arise to whisper to me: Here
comes the sun. Baby, you can drive my car. Oooh
you were meant to be near me. Take a sad song
and make it better and when I did, George held
my hand in the octopus's garden 'coz Something
in the way I moved attracted him like no other lover.

On The Way To Heaven

She nearly died the year before she
really died. I saved her, gave her
mouth-to-mouth, pounded her chest
like they do in the movies, bruising her,
until she finally came to, and, like in the
movies too, she smiled, looked around
and asked, "Where am I?" and when I told
my mother and that I'd saved her, she said,
Oh, no, you ruined everything. I was on my
way to heaven, heard angels singing. I was
dressed all in white and had no more pain.
She wept all morning.

In the afternoon she called me into her
bedroom and sternly told me that if that
ever happened again, not to save her.
I told her I couldn't help trying to
save her, that something stronger than
me made me do it, a reflex perhaps from
the womb like when she'd yank my hand
in time to save me from being run over by
a car. She screamed at me all afternoon
from her room how I'd ruined it for her
and would again and I screamed back how
sick I was of all this: the bedpans, the
morphine, my keeping her alive for her to
wish she'd die. Such ingratitude!
We both wept till dinnertime.

While I fed her dessert of vanilla ice cream,
my mother cleared her throat, letting me
know more was to come, but she apologized
instead, thanked me for saving her life.
"I know now how much you really must
love me," she said, "to save this old
bag of worthless bones." Then she laughed
for the first time in a long, long time.
I wanted to hug her, but I couldn't for
her pain. I'd never hug her, I knew,
ever again. But it felt good to both of us
when I cooled her bruises with a little
witch-hazel-soaked cotton swab.

Rick Smith

The Future

We eat cherry pie with our fingers
and lean against a 1953 Buick
gleaming in the heat.
I don't remember the other kid's name
but looking at the photographs
I know perfection
when I see it.

Writing in the dark,
embracing a false
but logical surface.
When lights go out
life goes on
and if you dip skin deep
into shadow and ink,
you only want more.

This is a blue room
and a girl sits at a yellow table.
Something like a tulip
is on the yellow table,
it seems to be on fire,
leaning over into red,
primary colors.

But it is thirst, wind
and cold that bring out
the hind brain best
where the hand does not waver,
but stays on the page
playing out the line
beyond any edges.

Poetry starts with a rope ladder
tossed into darkness
and what climbs up
lies before you, black.
It runs the border
in time lapse frames,
holds its breath
all the way
through
the Holland Tunnel,
walks out of Safeway

with a porterhouse steak
down its pants.

In my head, two telephones
are ringing and one of them
is always for me.
A voice says, "I can teach you
how to carry a grudge,
how to flourish
under the weight of luggage
without handles."

No, that's the wrong line.

I see a shooting star
and I pray for sanity.
My son pounds
fire caps on Jackson Street
in the Year of the Dog,
red on grey sidewalk.

This is the right line,
where magic turns dread
inside out.

Then there is thirst
and high wind
and sooner or later,
the rain gets to everyone.
But when I study the sky,
on the big screen,
in my near blindness,
I believe that the best
and the brightest
is still to come.

I believe men die dumb
and men die easy
in unanswerable
rain.

I believe if we live
long enough,
we will see our enemies
float by on the river,
if we live we will
eat cherry pie
with our fingers.

Barry Spacks

Dim Sum

I know, I know, if Ernest Hemingway
had savored the chicken bits
in piquant sauce
at the great Dim Sum Restaurant
in Monterey Park, California, he
still would have...could have...

or if Richard Brautigan
toward the withered end
had paused for the scallops at the Dim Sum
or ordered the platter of three
huge cream-filled dumplings, still he...
I know, I know, stupid thought,

but if only
John Berryman...Anne Sexton...
if Sylvia Plath...Primo Levi...
if Kathryn's father...
Robert Hazel...
if Marilyn Monroe...

Mike Sprake

Birds of Paradise Lost

My father's first vehicle was a Bantam
one twenty five cc. motorbike.

He'd ride it to work in all weathers
through the countryside
to the aircraft factory.

Over the years he brought three birds home
on the vinyl passenger seat.

The first a goose, much longer than I was.
Dad hung it by the feet
on the kitchen door hook.
Her neck stretched from the weight of the head
like a disabled pendulum
and blood dripped from the beak
into a pudding bowl on the floor.

The second bird arrived
in a pierced cardboard box
tied on with a sisal seat belt.
It must have been August;
my sister unwrapped him on her birthday.
She named the blue budgie, Mickey.
He became a family member for ten years—
sat in my hands while I watched TV,
till the day when mum found him spread eagle
on the cage floor amongst
the millet and seed husks.

The third was road kill.
A brown plump pheasant
full feathered;
plucked off a country lane
on the way home from work.
His feathers iridescent and worthy
of adorning an Austrian's alpine hat.

My mother spoke about how *gamey* they taste.
How when she worked as maid
for a lord in Yorkshire
the birds were hung till they began to decay
then eaten.

Those days of riding his Bantam ended
when my father bought his first car—
a blue three speed Ford Prefect
with pneumatic wipers
that labored across the windshield
when going up hills.

That's the time he lost his job
building aircraft.
When the government's secret
wing dipping TSR2
was scrapped at Boscombe Down
and those days in paradise on the airstrip
watching part of his creation take flight
were gone.

David St. John

Saffron

Even the thin tube of Spanish saffron
Sitting on the spice rack above the butcher block
Cooking table seems to glow with the worth
Of at least its weight in gold and today
At the beach a dozen Buddhist monks in golden
Robes stepped out of three limousines
To walk their Holy One out along the dunes

To the water's flayed edge where the sand burned
With a light one could only call in its reddish
Mustard radiance the essence of saffron
And what I remember most of the scene as
The Holy One knelt down to touch those waves
Was his sudden laughter and his joy and that
Billowing burnt lemon light opening across the sky

David Starkey

Lawnmower

So lazy that long ago summer, I had it coming. Dad had been after me all day to cut the grass
and clean the living room. *Just two goddamn things*, he swore before slamming shut my
door, *that's all I ask*. But I was busy back then with my Zeppelin records and phone calls
to my girlfriend, Pet. I let it slide.

I was so wasted last night, Pet was moaning during our third conversation of the morning, when
a bomb detonated downstairs. *What's that!* Pet yipped, but I'd already dropped the
receiver, started toward the noise, a raspy roar that hadn't stopped.

From the landing I saw Mom and my sister standing on the sofa, holding hands and screaming as
Dad wheeled the lawnmower across our thick gold shag. It took me several moments to
absorb. He'd set the wheels as low as they could go, so the carpet itself, not just my rock
star magazines, *Creem* and *Rolling Stone*, my unfinished homework, my paper plates of
half-eaten snacks, the soda cans, the junk mail I was saving to sort through someday, all
of it came shooting from the blower into the air like grass.

Carl! Mom yelled, *Carl, Carl, stop!* but he was starting on a footstool when my sister, who later
became a nurse, leapt and pulled the sparkplug wire. The roaring guttered out.
Nothing—but the air conditioner's hum, two kids playing outside.

I came down, silent, and began picking up the mess. Mom put her arms around her husband.
My sister went upstairs. I was nearly finished when I glanced over and saw him crying,
the one thing he'd told me a boy could never do. Mom, mascara running, hissed, angrier
than I'd ever heard her: *Not a word from you, mister. Not a word until you understand.*

Terry B. Stevenson

My Mother's Next Life
> For my mother, Phyllis.
> (1919-1993)

She doesn't believe in reincarnation
but plays this game for me
if it makes me feel better.

"Ok," she says:
"I would like to be reborn in the USA
the best country in the world
I want to come back as a man next time
I would be in show business
a dancer, the next Fred Astaire or Gene Kelly
there is no one like them now
I can't come back as Cary Grant
because then I would
be in love with myself."

I know she thinks this is a silly game
but it makes me feel better
to think that she is
at some kind of peace
with the fact that there's
less than a year to live.

I
would come back
as my
mother.

Karen Stromberg

To the Man in the Cul de Sac

I am sorry to hear
that you've lost your shoe.
It is four in the morning,
perhaps it has gone to bed.
Perhaps it grew tired of drinking,
and crawled under your couch.

Your neighbors,
lying awake in their dark beds,
wish it had never left you,
wish it would slip out of hiding
and carry you off
to wherever it is
you wish to go.

Pireeni Sundaralingam

Letters From Exile

These are the letters I leave behind me,
dull lines written for the censor's eye.
There are no stories here, only headlines,
statements of fact shielding the truth.

But how can I write my life without politics
when each word placed is part of an equation?
Talk of my income will be translated
into an exact amount for blackmail or ransom;
talk of our culture will be interpreted
as a covert call to arms.

I cannot tell you
that I am learning our language,
that I stand as a poet on a Western stage
crying out the loss of our country.

I cannot send you
photographs or cassette tapes.
You will not see my hair turn gray
or my voice change accent
as I become American.
I cannot even send you postcards
because such pictures
are considered currency in our country
and will go home with the postman
to be traded for food.

I will write these words for you
knowing the line of people that stand between us:
my cousin who will sit beside you, translating,
the villagers hoping for news of their families,
and the government clerk who will slit open
this letter, like all the others,
checking each word, over and over,
the most sensitive audience I could ask for.

Eileen Tabios

Latin

The necklace of rubies was an introduction. He thought to surprise her with a proposition. But she replied, *I have never liked my men on their knees!* He mustered a stand, blinking at the sunrays striking the crimson gems she was intently inspecting. Finally, she said, *I prefer my stones harder.* But he knew as he walked away forlornly that had he given her diamonds there still would have been no guarantees. Worst, he could feel her gaze on his back and it lacked enmity.

In his absence, she reached for a decanter and stained a crystal glass into amber. For a pensive moment, she held the crystal towards the generous light from a brass chandelier. She thought once more of her hidden desire: to freeze time around her, even if she must become a poor creature trapped in a honey-colored casket. For she has trained men to kneel and she is replete. *Fit in dominata servitus. In servitude dominatus.* But she coughed over her first swallow and recoiled at being surprised.

Then she reared at her reflection in the mirror. A stain was spreading across her shoulder. She reached for it and her uncontrolled gesture elongated its darkness across white, raw silk. The fabric wrapped around her breasts began to feel less than the price she paid for it. She had reached for it in SoHo's chicest boutique where she was waited on by a slim, tall man fearlessly dangling a thin moustache. The glimmer had compelled a memory of a lightning bolt cracking a summer night in New Mexico. She had reached for it and been surprised when her fingers touched something tangible that she thought was a bright light. And as the Kentucky whiskey continued to torture the silk, she began to consider whether she should attempt something else. Perhaps sweetness.

Phil Taggart

Alive in a New Millennium – Part 2

young lovers walk
around a homeless
man sprawled across
the sidewalk
on a hot Southern
California day.
I'm driving by;
driving home to spend
time with my daughter
and son-in-law visiting
from up north.
He's perched in front of
a virtual chess board
and she is off on
a walk so I settle
down with a book
and the book tells me:
the last 50 years of
our history had nothing
to do with a struggle
for peace, justice or
freedom but actually boils
down to the negotiations
of the degree of a mutually
acceptable violence.

Ambika Talwar

Naked Geometry—I

I begin to understand something
about the way honey seeks its home
that you need the mystery of arousal,
that you need the mystery of machismo

so you play the conqueror
before she has even come to you.

But what of the mystery of familiarity?
The strangeness of knowing a voice,
how it moves in between spaces.
The intricacy of smell that changes
from corner to curve past possibilities,
the valleys that take you to a place
beyond anything you can imagine

where the phoenix fires the cauldron
night after night after night
and where you drop your albatross
to renew its longing for a new poem
or invention of the mind or mettle—

like old hoary Hephy fashioning himself
with his tools, his constant going to and fro
hammering out his past on a template
of his future and losing himself
in his forgetfulness.

I begin to understand that forgetting
is a way to bypass a response,
that running all over is a way to lose
the road back home—to our beginnings

Chris Tannahill

Suicide Gene

While you sleep,
I drag jet streams across the moon.
My love in a remorseless orbit
around your bed.
Everything is blown to a black shade of blue,
pulling the road under your car,
sky up over head
like flames leaping freeways.

What a beautiful dance
that wears your hair in all directions.
Keeps me longer than evening.

While you sleep,
I pull the tide up to your door,
leave silt, shell, black starfish & coral
because I can't afford flowers sometimes.

We break under the weight
of too much meaning,
too much chaos;
it's horrible to have a talent for terrible things,
because in my world,
what you fear,
usually happens to you;
you see,
I was born with a suicide gene.
It kept saying,
"The world is gin and she wants everything."
But who cares for a fair fight anyway?
For how would I know
with vision like mine.

So give me a phrase,
anything. I'll twist it,
difference of an 's'
as we either,
Exit or exist;
oh, I was living in the house that Cuervo built
and baby, it was all a blur and without stars.

I can be the last thing you need,
worst way to breathe,
dropping acid, when I'm too lazy to re-decorate,
and by every impulse convinced, of all these strangers
as drapery; so I took my pain to a pawnshop
and with the cash,
bought an old Cadillac,
hell, everyone's selling something.
Violence, religion.
I gave it all up for humanity,
for a dress full of red wine.

Sometimes I just want your hands for
bookends, your skull for a paperweight,
bones on the Interstate.

I should have stuck with the Greeks,
who believed pearls exploded into being
when lightning struck the sea.

Now they pound the ground
from 65,000 feet
whispering words like,
Kabul, Kosovo, Cancer.
It's never a fair fight.
It's a suicide gene.
It's me once I stop speaking.

Judith Taylor

Only You Can Prevent Forest Fires

To live overpowered, devoted to my brilliant mistakes.
Every woman needs one Mr. Wrong in her life.
For emergencies, a cocktail of Valium and white wine.
Teetertottering toward stiletto assignations.
Bed of spikes, bed of fur, bed of silk—is there any difference?
I look to find things to dislike about Mr. Wrong: the grease on his tie,
        the worn-down heels of his klutzy brown shoes.
When Anna Karenina stares down that train, I want to yell, stop honey,
        no man is worth it!
I believe this six out of every seven days.
What is fiction, but another kind of mirror?

Keren Taylor

Control

I see my reflection in Pinocchio's nose—
it has grown so long that I polished it,
carved a landscape in its side.
That's my boy—tell me another lie
so I can add Malibu next to Santa Monica.
Just keep on lying and the entire west coast
will grace your face, you goddamn liar.
Oh, you can cry all you want to,
but you can't help lying
and I will keep carving the country
in your flesh
until you resemble nothing
except Rand McNally
and when I am done carving,
you will stop talking
and lie still.

Susan Terris

Self-Portrait In Wool

In magnetic air, my self or shadows of it,
the body a ballast for the head,
as I, red mask dragging an afghan body,
knit a new face from cosmic wool.

A three-dimensional life is formed by attitude.

Others want what I have, so I must sheer
invisible sheep, comb and card
the fleece, twist the thread, ply needles,
then teach them how to do the same.

All done with mist and a mirror or two.

Still, they can't expect to touch flesh.
This wool is thin, soft but without affect
and, its anxious thread tugged by
an unseen hook, keeps on unraveling.

Lynne Thompson

Seed of Mango, Seed of Maize

One of the grandmothers I only saw once
in a photograph.
She was short & sturdy, a black black Carib
with a forehead as wide as the sea
that kisses Port Elizabeth
and a nose broad as the nostrum of Admiralty Bay.
She seemed to be breathing deeply
and her breath was coconut and allspice,
mango and frangipani,
black bird and blue sky,
was the isle of Bequia.
She breathed a daughter,
then another daughter
and they breathed
5 daughters between them
and I am one of those flying fish.

The other grandmother I composed
from myth and half-told stories.
She was a red red Cheyenne—
scorched earth,
much chased,
sported a thick reed of braid to shade her back,
pulled off from her forehead
wide as Dakota
before it was north and south.
She whispers across ten, then 10 times
ten more years. She whispers
to a son who whispers to me
in my dreams, sometimes in my waking.
She comes as flute, blue maize, dance of the sun,
crow on the wing singing up the ghosts,
and I am one of those, a ghost, singing.

Mary Langer Thompson

Silence Across the Sideyards
For Diane

The eve of your daughter's wedding
I am drawn toward home.
I park in front
of where we used to live.
Two houses,
side by side,
repeopled, remodeled,
remembered.

Fresh from Chicago
we moved in.
California, 1956.
Dad cleaned and scrubbed,
unable to find work.
Mom took a job at Citizen's Bank.

Tired of Our Miss Brooks
and Mr. Ed's peanut buttered palate,
I wandered outside
dissolving a grape fizzy on my tongue.
There you were,
ten years old with blonde braids.
Of course your eyes were blue,
and we hula-hooped
from strangers to sidekicks.

You taught me to polka
down your hallway,
past your room
directly across from mine.
Soon I started to whistle
across the sideyards
whenever I had news.
You would appear,
see me
curlered and Clearasiled.

After school we'd dance
to American Bandstand.
Overnight, we'd ride Route 66
to see Steve Allen.

You learned to drive first.
Of course your car was blue.

A whistle
and soon a light
to share moments from dates,
while your dog, Lucky,
paced beneath our windows.

Between learning and teaching
we married.
I stood in your wedding—
(of course my dress was blue)
and you in mine.
We birthed our babies
a month apart.
Yours will marry tomorrow.

The disease
bombarded your blood
and took you quickly.
Within three days.
We buried you in blue.

A woman now collects
autumn leaves,
and rose petals,
like tears,
lie on the lawn.
I strain to hear
a whisper of a whistle,
but all I hear is
silence across the sideyards.

Paul Trachtenberg

Nurse! Nurse!

Homeostatis is too long
to serenade ars poetica.
Never-the-less, the place
is preferable than having
hormones raiding organs
for their complacencies.

Who says that laconic lyricism
can not be structured from
multi-syllabic protein?
Words are thick salamis
topped with various cheeses.

Nurse! Nurse! Stitch-up my
spleen from leaking hysteria
all over my bedazzled person.
Seamless bewilderment rules
while writing on this wall.

Oh nurse! The cerebrum,
in which I stand, take my pen
and cadence the wall
with a soothing remedy.

Ben Trigg

Wet

He had eyes to drown in:
underwater labyrinths, coral mazes
leading away from everything you'd ever known or trusted.
You ran,
took corners so fast you were on two wheels,
crashed into wall after wall.
He held you like a snake-charmer turning from reptiles to polished glass.
He led you in circles and squares, led you in so many shapes,
turned you inside out;
obsidian, obscured, beautiful.
You let him sculpt,
shape you so light refracted,
every color imaginable pouring from your body,
blinding the infidel who dared to look.
He revealed in you a holiness only his eyes could comprehend.
"Eyes to drown in," you said,
leading to a place of understanding where breath was currency.
Eyes so deep you grew gills,
left behind those of us who couldn't swim.

Duane Tucker

The Old Stone House

The morning after I left for the last
time, I walked the river in the rain, pondering the half
century I'd called it home. The dandelion days
of books and badminton and squirt guns and now this:

a prison of wrinkles and recrimination, pills and walkers. I stared
at the river and it became the Susquehanna, silver and slow
behind the white-washed house where my grandparents
summered. The house that gave birth to the stone

house: half its contents ours and most of the family's reverence
for language. Soon the house would be gone and my parents
with it. Gone the grandfather clock whose chime was my
childhood. Gone the portrait of Grandpa that had hung over

the fireplace ever since I could remember. Gone the little
walnut chair he had given me at 4.
The chair I'd treasured everywhere—even to bed.
I remembered tiptoeing up to his study,

easing the door open to sit on it and peek.
I was forbidden to disturb him—but how could I
help it. He caught me. Instead of scolding, he boosted
me into his lap, acrid-honey of King Sano's on his vest.

He let me try his fountain pen—smeary
thrill of the scratch-marks I made on his yellow
legal pad like touching a bird's wing, kissing a blue-
eyed girl. He gave me a piece of salt-water taffy and bundled me

off to walk by the river. For a concrete kid to August
in woods and wasps, corn and minnows
was bliss beyond
words; was the reason I adored these walks in the rain.

And now this
rain was that rain: impervious
cows carpet-sweeping the fields, the fieldstone walks
freckled with leaves and after, the stars

bobbing like fields of chicory. And I saw in the eager mouths
the rain opened in the river how water adores
the prodigal. How nothing is ever lost but not seeing
the blazing and unbroken circle that never stops giving.

Kathleen Tyler

Last Gift

On the film sheet, the lump looks like a galaxy. A white
mass with reticulated ends spinning through negative space.

You come to know the language it whorls
after itself: *in situ, noninvasive, metastasized;* and all
its stages, as though it has learned to sit, bounce
a ball, strap on skates.

Things your mother taught you.

Rocking on a swing
in the play area of a drive-in movie,
your head tilted, sneakers dragging sand.

"Name the constellations," you insisted,
"start with the Hydra."

Last time you saw her well, she was deadheading
hybrid tea roses, her clippers punctuating air.

As if to say, *they demanded too much.*

Finally, you are close to her. Brought together on a field
of wildly reproducing cells. You will regard with similar
mystification the surgeon's strange, violet hieroglyph marking
your own breast: this is how we die. Circling the nipple, the swollen,
purple areola, a word so like aureole: the radiance crowning saints.

"Do not ask the names of things," she said,
"love only their light, their form."

Amy Uyematsu

I'm Old Enough To Know Better

To recognize that stupid smile
just before he asks,
"Do you teach the Korean class?"
He thinks he's getting one step closer
in the friendly nods we namelessly
exchange at work.
"I'm not Korean, I'm Japanese."
I wait to see how he'll react,
watching his half-open
mouth as he fumbles for words
and hoping he suffers
just a little embarrassment,
but just my luck
he's an unconscious
stockpile of insults—
"Well, I'm just a round-eye,"
and he walks off grinning,
not even suspecting what
damage he's done for all
the "round-eyes" of this world.

It's my own fault
for trusting a town
where Asian faces are almost
as common as hearing Spanish
and it surely feels safe enough
to walk on hip San Vicente
among those who love sushi,
dig yoga and Zen.

But I'm way too old
not to have seen the next one
coming, only two weeks later.
Three guys in suits, maybe tourists,
one looks at me as if we've met before.
Just as we pass
on that Brentwood sidewalk,
he leans toward me,
beaming, in broken English—
"Oriental massage, good."
The sad truth is,
he meant it
as a compliment.

Ann Vermel

Valerie's Dam

When she tells me about the afternoon she built the dam
some mother-bond in my body lets me feel it—the water
pulling at her calves, running through her toes clear green
over sand and pebbles twisting through willow roots,
the lengthening sun on her back and the weight of stone.
I see, too, how she gauges progress, assesses design
how those long strong legs straddle her universe,
and small rivers bend to her will.
The sound of the afternoon stream clatters quietly
in my heart, lifting out of the current her grandmother's voice
to tell us both how ancient Romans placed their stones,
shaped waterways, built empires, how it is good
that her daughters stand in the live green current
among the small, perfect fishes,
building.

Fred Voss

Poetry in the Hammered Air

Do I not have a hundred poets around me
in this factory?
Throwing down the back gates of their trucks at lunch
to scream, "EEEEHOLA!" and spit
on asphalt and bare their teeth at each other shouting
about women and tequila
and car engines
wearing spotless felt fedora hats as they dip brass parts
into fuming tanks of solvent all day
looking
at red sunsets over L.A. skyscrapers through machine heads
and compressed air pipes and rolled-open tin doors
they sweat
down their back and wave their arms
in rolled-up sleeves and dream of crap tables in Laughlin
and beautiful Mexican girls walking down broadway
and old
Civil War pistols and plaster
their toolboxes with pictures of boxers who are afraid
of nothing was there ever
poetry
if it is not in their eyes as they stride toward their cars
at quitting time in each fingertip
they have managed not to cut off after a lifetime
next to razor-sharp steel edges
who
will ever write a better poem that the tattoos
on the backs of their necks
or the lines
on their hands weathered and carved with the sliding
of a million bars of steel
off the backs of flatbed trucks?

Lizzie Wann

Aero-Dynamics

he likes to know what the sky is doing
to understand the movement of wind
its origin or its destination
how it sweeps down from Alaska into California
and over to Texas
brings winter

when it approaches
he wants to know if he should keep his door locked against it
or maybe leave the door ajar, to let whatever forces come in
or if he should swing it open wide
so the winds have to cross his threshold
to get where they're going
re-shape his living in the process

he is aware of air traffic over Los Angeles
lights line the sky
mark a pattern of arrival
against fixed outlines of myths

he notices shapes of clouds
how they are lit from western sunlight
points them out to me as a reminder of everyday poetry

he curves his arm around my waist
like the arc of a plane on final approach

Scott Wannberg

The War

had its grandchildren over for the afternoon.
They looked at the scrapbook,
smiled, told one another jokes, ate well...
The War told everyone it was going to wear brand new clothes
but if you look close enough
the labels are angrily familiar...
The War knows where to buy food cheap
but good stuff nonetheless...
The War had a drinking problem
but it got smart, joined AA
nothing but coffee now...
The War came over to my apartment this afternoon
to borrow a video.
I don't know if I should loan the War any of my things
It usually loses them, forgets to return anything...
The War got on its knees and prayed for more victims
before turning in.
Dear God, the War said, please let me go on and on and on
I am enjoying myself.
The War is getting younger all the time.
Nobody should look that young.
Nobody.

James Michael Warren

Crayons

After giving my four-year-old a box
of crayons in sixty-four brilliant hues,
I ask her what colors she prefers.
She tells me she likes blue and green.
These are the colors of the sky and trees.

I point out the periwinkle, turquoise,
aquamarine, and cadet-blue as alternatives.
I lift up the forest, olive, spring, and sea greens
to compete with the green she's drawn,
but she overrules me.

Later, she shows me a blue-green stick-figure
standing in a field beside a tree
that looks like it's about to topple.
That's you Daddy! she yells.

I look at her hazel eyes and want to trap
her innocent enthusiasm in my hug.
All too soon she'll be choosing shades
of sepia, salmon, raw umber, and maize,
with no guidance from me.

Salt Licks

When I pour the crystals over my stew,
she says I use too much. She says
my arteries will harden like stone, and
I'll look back, one day, to find that
my blood is frozen in the pillar I've become.

She frowns when I relate my childhood flights
down through the cholla cactus and Joshua trees
to the goat's pen, with its juniper shade, where
I ran my pink tongue over the salty-smooth
depressions mined into their crystalline cakes.

Why would anyone want to lick salt and goat spit?
She shudders at the thought and edges
the salt shaker out of my reach. I want to tell her
that my craving carries over from the quest
to weigh my worth against its bitter taste.

So I start to stutter, trying to describe
the palimpsest scars of a father's belt-buckle-bite,
and she weeps with my frustration. And I lean in
to kiss away the dampness on her cheek,
already savoring the salt caught in her tears.

Charles H. Webb

The New World Book of Webbs

> *"I have exciting news for you and all Webbs."*
> —Miles. S. Webb

The brochure shows a boat passing the Statue of Liberty
while its cargo of immigrants stand gaping,
and one small boy—dressed better than the rest—
watches from a director's chair. He,
obviously, is the Webb. Simple but aristocratic.
Poor, but destined for greatness. Set apart

from the Smiths and Joneses, the Rothblatts
and Steins, the Schmidts and Hampys, the Mancusos
and Malvinos and Mendozas and Tatsuis
and Chus, by "the distinguished Webb name."
Excitement steams from Miles S. Webb's letter to me.
The very type leaps up and down. Just buy

his book, and I will learn (I'm guessing)
about Thomas Webb, famous for his kippered
herring jokes, and Dan Webb of the talking armpits,
and Genevieve Webb, convinced her left
and right feet were reversed. I'll learn the inside story
of Solomon Webb, Dover's greatest circus geek,

and Lady Messalina Webb, transported to Australia
with her husband, Sir Caleb Webb,
son of the merkin-maker Jemmie Webb of Kent.
Best of all, inside the bonus *Webb International Directory*,
one among 104,352 Webb households in the world,
there I'll be: the very Webb who woke this morning

at 5:53 when his new sprinklers ratcheted on
with the screech of strangled grebes—the Webb
who lay in bed hearing the artificial rain, then cracked
his drapes and saw fat drops annoint his porch,
and a hummingbird light on a hair-thin twig,
then buzz away when the sprinklers hissed off.

The lawn lay drinking, then—each blade
with its own history, each listed in the Book of Heaven
(Grandma Webb from Yorkshire used to say),
each destined to be cut later this morning by José,
one of 98,998 people to bear (his letter states)
the "brave and glorious name Cortez."

Florence Weinberger

Measured for Love

Fiddling with the view finder to get a fix on you, I found you dwarfed next
to a mountain. A Small crown in back, pebbles at your foot would have lent you heft.
I still had choices. Black and white film would have marbled your left

side and helped texture the half-light where the wide brim of your hat
kept the sun off your neck and your slightly averted cheek; instead of getting that
dappled pattern, I used Kodak Gold to gild your skin, fringe of gray hair, the sexual

insolence of those wrap-around sunglasses that seemed to exalt your vision
like some desert lizard effortlessly camouflaged against disaster.
The film developed, I am shown the rest, from lens to earth to horizon: frozen

shoulders, arms inert at your sides, a tongue asleep in a mouth without trust,
knees locked like a prisoner's. Indifferent as a billboard, you snubbed
me. I see how you refused to be measured full length for love.

I see how every rock behind you gained in majesty by its casual reach, and a few
trees, especially the ones repeatedly grazed by the wind, achieved a lasting beauty
which I caught by happenstance, while I was looking somewhere else. At you.

I see how desire implicated my right hand. I see how the camera fought me
when I forced open its shuttered eye. I see your disgust. I see my despair.
I see how shadow sucked in whatever came close. The end of the affair.

David Weinreb

Mom

At a skinny scared sixteen there was a mystery
Walking around under her bloody white slip
On Swinney industrial street grey and grim
Various furtive glances at that black thatch
Her boyfriends got it all the time
Fat assed Ron donut smashing Jerry
Married Bud with overhauls hillbilly Dewey with big feet
I hated my ignorance she couldn't explain
No father around off in improvisation
Shoveled walks returned her worn shoes
Did a pseudo dad with the younger kids
A blindfolded sex drive she was just living
Now I walk the want it all the time walk
Which can never take care of me like she did
All beautiful and thin and smoking and sad

Patricia Wellingham-Jones

Indelible Ink

I stole mulberries from the mockingbirds
off the tree bending over the ditch,
carried the black fruit home cupped
in the warm bowl of my palm.
Served them on a small square white tray
on the deck with morning coffee
and watched our lips, teeth, hands
and shirtfronts turn purple with juice.
I saw Mother's long ago frowns
when I raced home dotted with ink
from climbing our neighbor's mulberry tree
and me cramming handfuls
of the dark sweet fruit into an eager mouth
in those days when mulberries
were sweeter than kisses.

Jackson Wheeler

Photograph: A Poem Written For My Mother On a Line From Dickinson

This autumnal sky is wide and pale.
You stand in your winter garden
Hoe in hand, among collards, turnips, kale,

Turning away from the camera I hold.
The shadow of your house forms a margin,
A darker metaphor perhaps. I am told

You find work to bend to each day.
My photograph of you is a temporary pardon,
We both linger where we cannot stay.

You have grown old; I am older
And we'll soon know all there is to know of Heaven,
As the days grow shorter, the air turns colder.

Leigh White

Before Our Faces Begin To Sag

My soul became a pet rock
that no one wanted,
so it had to be put to sleep
at the humane society.

Texas got this hairball the size of Texas
and couldn't stop coughing up blood money.

Someone
put on too much cologne
and it smelled like the longest day
you ever had at work.

There were piles of powder
here and there
shaped like little Gizas,
meaning that someone had just
thrown up.

I ponder my choices.
Do I forgive my parents
for dropping me as a baby...

Bruce Williams

Poems My Family Really Doesn't Like

My wife's not crazy
about most changes I make
between a first
and second draft.

(I'm her third husband,
she's my first wife.)

She hates cute remarks
like those I've just made,

along with poems
that shred her privacy
and anything
which shows I've read James Tate.

My daughter despises every poem
with names she doesn't know—
like James Tate.

She loathes the ones
that say that she's like me—
with her fierce dramatic eyes
and mention bad habits we both share.

Grandma
likes everything
but she's ninety-one
and polite.

And the cat?

Fortunately Spike has never read
the pantoum
where the cat gets kicked
and thrown
out in the rain.

But she dislikes
anything that interrupts my petting hand
so she jumps on my desk

and sheds grey hair
on everything I write.

And what bothers me—
as dressing in the dark
and finding later
not just socks
but shoes don't match?

This poem.
And all my poems
that stop instead of end.

M.L. Williams

Bone Wine

Unpruned vines bend to earth
Early winter in Paso Robles,
When rain spills into the chalk
And loam between black roots and fists
Of antediluvian bone.
I found, set beside a black oak's
Mossy trunk, one hacked vertebrae,
Gone to mineral and grey as paper
All these million years. The bone
Drank up the downpour, or seemed to,
Thirsty from holding up all dead
And living ages of the dust.

I brought it home ten years ago,
And now I drink the wine that grows there,
Hold up the glass to watch the living
Light shimmer, and keep a hallowed place
To rest the used up fossil, save it
Like a river stone. But my grandfather,
Himself now bone and paper,
He'd have kicked it into the vines,
Cursed at it, scolded, "Get back to work."
And it would've.

Paul Willis

First Rain

falls the morning before Halloween, cold and thick.
I interrupt my eight-o'clock to drive downtown
for jury duty, park five blocks away, leap and dodge
the swollen gutters to join a swirl of citizen peers.
Three of them I recognize: a local physical therapist
who is also a famous rock climber, a neighbor who teaches
computer science at city college, and an elder poet
from the university. Sunday, he stood in our kitchen
and read us his poem about the September 11 attacks,

a poem on the model of "This is the house that Jack built,"
a poem full of maidens all forlorn. But I am wrong
about the neighbor. She is actually a more distant
acquaintance, an artist whose husband manages
our retirement funds: I would make a better juror
than a witness. During a break, the climber tells me
about his latest, a 5.11 spire to the north of Whitney—
a route so far beyond my skill it fails to stir
my latent envy. Is this the meaning of middle age?

I wish him well, recall that once he broke his back
on talus at the foot of Half Dome. Because of his own
ailing back, the elder poet gets a deferral. The climber
somehow falls away, the artist brushes past me
for another courtroom. Outside, the rain makes
bubbles on the parking lot under a pepper tree,
and the rest of us spread out like rainbowed streaks of oil,
awaiting our chance at some small justice, the solace
of autumn, the hallowing of a dark new year.

Cecilia Woloch

Custom

> *"This is no dark custom"* —*Gertrude Stein*

Some days you wake up and find god in your shoes and you don't know who put it there. Or the little gold clocks in your irises, or the long stems of sun on your desk. So you just dress in coffee and beautiful rags and be glad of it, ashes and all. And you hum to yourself some ridiculous tune that sounds like a handkerchief stuffed in your mouth. Which means that you won't get a single thing done, oh no not today, but your papers don't mind. They lie around like wanton brides and admire you anyway. Fat apples blossom in baskets left on your table; wine turns into wine. And the windows, my god the windows have gathered absurd amounts of sky. *If the shoe fits, the foot must be mine.* Someone who loves you dreamed double last night.

Sholeh Wolpé

Butcher Shop

Aisha was gunned down
in her father's butcher shop.
She was twenty-four, a virgin,
has a cat named Hanna.

The boys in black bandanas,
the ones with large dark eyes
that devour light
wanted her brother.

And what better place for blood
than in a butcher shop
where it already covers the counters,
stains the white aprons,
is sold in long red sausages.

Robert Wynne

San Francisco Suite

1. Arrival

The moon shines off the waves.
I only know the sand is there
because I can't see it.
After more than 7 hours of driving
this dark coast marks
the beginning of the long weekend.
Cecilia's got at least ten friends
to see. I just need to see something
other than Los Angeles. I take her
to Jorge's and he hands us drinks,
makes a late dinner. I am hungry.
As soon as the wine flushes my tongue,
with the smell of onions and garlic
already filling the room, I have forgotten
the shape of the steering wheel,
the sprawling city we've come from,
the woman I haven't been able to keep
out of my mind.

2. Falling Sky

for Jorge Argueta

You are on a binge again:
1 bottle of tequila, 8 beers,
bottle after bottle of wine.
You haven't slept in 2 days,
and when someone tells you
to lay down, you say, "No pendejo!"
If I close my eyes
the sky's gonna fall on me!
The sky's gonna swallow me up
and take me away."

How can I tell you
the sky is nothing
but a dream of earth and water,
like our bodies?
Only the sky is big enough
to contain us, each of us,
a body of water walking the earth.

3. Heart

San Francisco is heart-shaped—
the human heart, not one of those
pink Valentine cut-outs.
From the top of the Fairmont Hotel,
I watch cars course across bridges
away from this compact miracle
of a city. Here there is no room
for anything unnecessary.
I miss Deb. For a moment
I am consumed again
by the peculiar loneliness of loving
someone who can't love you
back. For a moment I want to jump,
crash through the plate glass
and make a place for myself
on the crowded surface below.

4. Houses

At Robert's place, the window faces
streets overrun by homes.
Not even an inch separates them.
So many houses are ugly
in this beautiful city.
They squat like lettered blocks
on the floor of a child's room.
What word is she spelling,
this girl who doesn't realize
she is creating the world
with such tiny hands?

5. The First Annual Dinner of the Bay Area
   Chapter of the Friends of Cecilia

We gather at Saigon Saigon
in the Mission District. Some have never met;
some haven't seen each other in a long time.
I've never had Vietnamese food before,
and as the eggplant stuffed with seafood
in a coconut sauce slides down my throat,
I wonder why. Anne sits in her electric chair
at the end of the table, trying
to get her son Max to eat
more than just chicken dishes.

Mario and Uschi are marveling
at the New Zealand Zinfandel.
Jorge and Teresa are nibbling and talking
about the dinner they had earlier.
Ken is explaining why all the best restaurants
are family operations like this one.
Tonight's agenda: eat, drink, talk.
At our next meeting, we'll elect officers,
draft a charter and take up a collection
to buy a bottle of 1971 Chateau Margeaux.
No one is taking minutes, and no one knows
quite how we all came together
on what is just another evening for Cecilia.
Outside the restaurant, we are so loud when we part
passing drivers pull over to see what's going on.
How can we tell them all we want
is to take the love in each other's eyes
home to keep us company?

6. Love Poem to a Friend

for Cecilia Woloch

I drop you off late
after too much wine.
I kiss you on the lips.
Inside, you tuck yourself
into bed. Maybe tonight you'll dream
of me singing,
with the voice I reserve
for all those I love,
whom I will never love.
Pull the borrowed covers of this night
tight to your chin. The dark sky fills
the window of your room.
The moon is an empty hammock.

7. Luna

Luna is 8 years old.
She is a force of nature already
like her namesake in the night sky.
She walks into her father's house,
picks up a portable CD player
and says, "Papi! Can I have this?"
What can Jorge do but give it to her?

Teresa looks for the headphones.
Luna scolds her Papi for cussing
then climbs out a window onto the roof.
It is Jorge's day to see his daughter.
They are going to the park,
but not until she is done
instructing the wind, the clouds
from her perch here
at the bottom of the sky.

8. The Labyrinth

At Grace Cathedral, I take my shoes off
and walk onto the labyrinth woven
into the carpet. I remember wanting
to write a poem about this
after my last lover had come here
and told me she'd found something in this exercise.
I wonder what Michelle found. I wonder
what it felt like when she reached the center.
Perhaps she stood in silence with her hands pressed together
as this red-haired man does now. Perhaps she didn't pause
for fear she'd lose the way back to her life.
I slide into the center
past this man who's heading out
into the new world
he's found there.
I feel no different.
From this white circle,
surrounded by a path with no choices,
I watch bright shafts fall
through picturebook windows
to stain the floor with the face of Jesus.
And I hear Deb laughing
at the gullibility of light,
how it can be made to tell any story.
I see her face everywhere:
the altar of the virgin, the modest statue
of Eve tucked in a corner, the apostle
brilliant in colored glass
whose halo contains the setting sun
five minutes each day.
I have found only my familiar life
in this labyrinth, a vision of a past
I can't seem to leave behind, and the quiet shuffle
of my feet on someone else's path.

Stepping off the carpet, I turn and bow
to this map of corners
so many have crossed.
Then I strap on my shoes,
go back outside and keep moving.

9. Silence

Jorge hands me the phone.
He says silence wants
to have a word with me.
I hold the quiet handset to my ear,
listen intently and nod
but say nothing.
Sometimes that's all you can do.

10. Bridge

Sunday I can't sleep. I am too busy
denying desire for a woman 500 miles away
who spends her days with God
instead of me. I go outside
and have one last cigarette.
One more glass of wine.
I see the silhouette of a couple
making love on a patio.
He is holding her close
enough to deny any light
which could separate them.
Even the glow of one visible star
is lost in a sky too full with clouds
for the names of people, constellations.
Back inside I pull my clothes off slowly
and listen as the boxed matches
in my pocket rattle like tiny bones
shaken loose from a body small enough
to crush inside a fist. I crumple
my pants into a ball, lie down
knowing sleep will quiet my mind, knowing
this city will still be here in the morning—
glowing in the early fog
with the promise of a bridge strong enough
to carry me away.

Brenda Yates

Flora, Fauna and Genitalia

Eventually, it all comes down to sex. Wild
Roses exhaust themselves, aching with pollen,
Ovaries swell, ready to burst, to feed
Tiny mice, pink and blue-veined, squirming
In nests close to the snakes that crawl under
Cucumber vines near the pond where fish

Gorge on speckled slicks of frog spawn.
Adrift in the slow, summer heat, some
Ripen and tails quicken with sudden
Desire, tadpoles unfolding in the furious,
Elemental thrust to live,
Notwithstanding all this death.

Chryss Yost

Last Night

When the sun sets, and he isn't home, she walks
Not to be waiting, but she leaves a note:
Back soon, her only message, only wish.

After all, she didn't think he'd stay;
No plans, so no surprises when it ends.
The dishes wait unwashed. Bitter stains

Stretch like shadows on the tablecloth.
Once you believe in finding gods in mortal men
You understand their restlessness as faith;

The way she feels his truth against her skin,
The rough edge of a matchbook, while she grieves
To see her saviors lost, and lost again.

God save the church that she takes refuge in,
The sanctuary given fools and thieves,
This silent girl who loves a man who leaves.

Gary Young

Untitled

The signature mark of autumn has arrived at last with the
rains: orange of pumpkin, orange persimmon, orange lichen on
rocks and fallen logs; a copper moon hung low over the
orchard; moist, ruddy limbs of the madrone, russet oak leaf,
storm-peeled redwood, acorns emptied by squirrels and jays;
and mushrooms, orange boletes, Witch's Butter sprouting on
rotted oak, the Deadly Galeria, and of course, chanterelles,
which we'll eat tonight with pasta, goat cheese, and wine.

Andrena Zawinski

It Is Enough For Now

On the table where I pick through a toothy smiling
fish, I put aside my map marked for textiles south
to Flores. A slip of paper calls me with stories
of fortress promenades and Hemingway's haunt
in old Havana, sliced mango, whole strawberries,
sweet bursting on the tongue. I dream instead
up Puuc Hills, on the road, Uxmal ahead, reach
the doormouth of a raingod's hooknosed mask, scale
the pyramid of an egg-hatched dwarf until the sun
sets down and bush groans low and loud behind my back.

I hitch a ride to Merida, in the wrong direction,
rumble on until the *virgen* icon flashes, illuminates
diesel smoke at the dash. We break down. I think
I should have ridden the train into Guatemala,
should have taken the restaurant tour of Cuba.

Later at the hotel, I will panic the air, banter
about buses, boycotts, seizing public transportation.
When I get home, I will hear Guatemalans are still
afraid to claim their dead from civil road patrols,
hear Cubans float out on death rafts, hope cast
to the wind on the straits, that they take hostages
in Alabama to escape deportation.

For now, people rise up only to stand and stretch
in the aisle, watch the driver tinker with hammer
and wrench. No one gets off. No one asks questions.
For now, it is enough for me to get lost beneath
remaining light in a book of poems about living
somewhere else, explosives and identities hiding
under layers of everyday life. It is enough
for now to watch, to believe: something
must come of all this.

Essays

A MEANS OF TRANSPORT:
George Hitchcock & *kayak*

by Philip Levine

Aside from comic books, the first publication that obsessed me was *Life* magazine. I was probably only nine or ten when I discovered its riches, which were then available for a dime, a sum I could earn in an hour. No, it wasn't the politics or vision of Henry Luce, the booster of unrestrained capitalism, that grabbed me; the last thing I did was read the articles. It was the photographs, at first the war photographs from Spain & China & later those from Europe, North Africa, & the Pacific as well as the great photographic record of an America stumbling through the blighted peace of the depression with its bread lines, dust-bowl nightmares, & industrial cities going to ruin. Until I discovered the poetry of T.S. Eliot, the images of Robert Capa, Margaret Bourke-White, Dorthea Lange, Carl Mydans, Edward Clark, Alfred Eisenstaedt & their colleagues were the most powerful I knew. When in high school I got into poetry the word began to replace the photographic image, & by the time I discovered at eighteen "The Preludes" by T. S. Eliot the process was almost complete. Little wonder that two decades later I hit upon a magazine that fascinated me almost as much as *Life* had & certainly more than any other literary publication. It was, of course, George Hitchcock's *kayak*, the first poetry journal I knew that was dedicated to the image & the only one I've ever ransacked with the same feverish anticipation I had those early issues of *Life*. In the very first issue from a poet I'd never heard of, Louis Z. Hammer, I stumbled across, "Investigators are prying in the American bloodstream; / In Wyoming a horse dies by a silver river, / Two maiden sisters in Los Angeles have torn open their hands..." And from the editor himself,

> America, beneath your promise
> there are underground lakes
> full of morphine
> and broken carburetors!
>
> Doors open and close on my shadow.
> My intestines burn. I am expelled
> from various academies.

(The writing alone—even without the gas—would have gotten him expelled from any number of academies.) This was something new & different: it was neither the self-righteous rhetoric of the Thirties protest poetry nor the overheated rant of the literary victim. Impossible to locate its origins in the American poetry of the Forties & Fifties or English poetry since the fall. This was a surrealism, or better an ultra-realism, whose fathers & mothers were unleashed Americans & whose uncles were Europeans, Iberians, & Latin Americans. There's a myth that American poetry was asleep during the Eisenhower years; American poetry has never been asleep; however, the best known contemporary poetry during the post-war era was certainly powerfully sedated. The poets wild enough to be truly American were underground only because the official organs of reproduction were too sterile to allow them life anywhere else. What *kayak* did was collect these separate writers into a national movement & then sic them on the *Hudson* & *Sewanee* reviews.

All you had to do was look at the magazine to know it was something new. (It's been copied so often that today someone first stumbling upon it might not recognize how striking it was in 1964.) Bound in heavy cardboard & voluminously illustrated, it sold for only a dollar or three dollars for a two-year subscription of four issues. The paper itself had a crude substantiality, "target paper"—I was later told—that George got cheaply. The illustrations were mainly engravings taken from odd & magical sources. For example, *kayak* 2 was dedicated to America's Underground Channels & Seams & the engravings were mainly taken from *Boston's Main Drainage* (1888) & Andre's *Practical Coal Mining* (1879). Each issue bore the following motto as an indication to possible contributors & readers of what the magazine's ambitions were:

> A kayak is not a galleon, ark, coracle, or speedboat. It is a small
> watertight vessel operated by a single oarsman. It is submersible, has
> sharply pointed ends, and is constructed from light poles and the skins
> of furry animals. It has never yet been successfully employed as a
> means of mass transport.

If you hoped to appear in the magazine you had to paddle your own boat; where you were headed was your business. The epigones of Lowell & Wilbur were not welcome. From that first issue it was a place for me to discover new poets as well as a new vision of our poetry. It was here I first read John Haines, David Antin, Bert Meyers, Lou Lipsitz, Dennis Schmitz, Kathleen Fraser, Herbert Morris, Margaret Atwood, Charles Simic, Bill Knott, Margaret Randall, Adrien Stoutenberg, Shirley Kaufmann, James Tate, Adam Cornford, Steve Dunn, Mark Doty, William Matthews, Mark Jarman, & Brenda Hillman. Within a few issues well-known poets as diverse as Tom McGrath, David Ignatow, Louis Simpson, W.S. Merwin, John Logan, Wendell Berry, Hayden Carruth, Paul Blackburn, Donald Justice, Gary Snyder, Anne Sexton, Charles Wright, Raymond Carver, Stephen Dobyns, Charles Hanzlicek, Kenneth Rexroth, Peter Everwine, & Richard Hugo made appearances, & curiously none of them seemed in the wrong neighborhood: they sounded like themselves & like one of the voices of *kayak*. I can still recall Mark Strand telling me over thirty years ago, "I've got a poem coming out in *kayak*!" Clearly it had become the place to appear. I seriously doubt this was George's ambition for his eccentric journal, but for years the poets had been starved for just such a meeting space & finding it we found it irresistible. I haven't mentioned translations, which became a regular feature of the magazine. Except for Rexroth's superb versions of the Chinese they were largely of Twentieth century European poets not yet discovered by many Americans: Rafael Alberti, Benjamin Peret, Odysseus Elytis, Vincente Huidobro, Hans Mangus Enzensberger, Tomas Tranströmer, et.al.

By 1969 it had become a quarterly & was regularly publishing prose; not just prose poems—for they were there from the start—but prose-prose, critical essays, reviews, & visionary opinion pieces representing utterly conflicting views. The reviews could be tough, sometimes even tough on regular *kayak* poets. (I was one who got bombed, although as I recollect not as badly as Dan Halpern in a review titled "Short Order Cooks of Poetry" which savaged Halpern's anthology of the younger American poets.) And the letters. One must not forget the letters, for they became for many a source of great wonder. An early one from Shirley Kaufmann, a response to the Kayak Press book *Pioneers of Modern Poetry* edited by George and Robert Peters, brought to our attention an all but unknown though masterful poet, Alexander Raphael Cury, whose poem "Inquiring About the Way," Kaufmann demonstrated, had inspired Kafka, although the poem, unlike either *The Trial* or *The Castle*, ended on a note of hope:

I am going home.
Go home.

What is the name of this place?
Square
Street
Lane.

Equally delicious were the gripes. One from Rodney Nelson of San Francisco began:

I hope you will excuse me for being direct: I see no point in sending *Kayak* any more poems or articles. The fact that you, as editor, are free to interpose your own personality between me & the readers is a sure indication that your magazine is socially unhealthy... Why should an editor steal a stamped, self-addressed envelope from a writer... Because nothing else matters but sly harassment, when the world is falling down around your ears. Into this picture fit you & your incredibly silly magazine, neither of which would last a minute in a people's society...

If this was the idiocy George was getting from the left, it's hard to imagine how much worse the complaints from the right were. From the start *kayak* presented found poems. I don't believe they were there only for laughs. The poets of that era—perhaps the poets of every era—had a tendency to exaggerate their social & spiritual significance. There was a lesson here for all of us who hoped to survive the violence & pain of the Sixties: without a healthy & ribald disrespect for authority we were doomed. Like his great forebearer Walt Whitman in the preface to *Leaves of Grass*, George was telling us in his own writing & in the sassy & irreverent entity that was *kayak,* to take off our hats to no one.

I first met George Hitchcock in the spring of 1965. He'd come to Fresno as one of two poets reading on the Academy of American Poets California Circuit, which was then in its infancy. (Unfortunately it never lived into its teens.) The other poet was my old friend Henri Coulette. For the students at Fresno State it must have been something of an eye-opener; if they'd had any notions regarding the nature of the poet, his or her appearance, style, character, & writing, these two would have blown it. Henri was perhaps half a foot shorter than George & very slender—an ex-distance runner, he still looked as though he could do a mile in four minutes & change—. He dressed in the style of an under secretary of state on the threshold of a promotion: for day wear (& the reading took place in the early afternoon) he favored light gray suits, bright ties, ox-blood loafers. His dark hair was cut so short that its natural curliness was barely visible. His complexion was a light olive; he was, he claimed, in spite of his name a "black Irishman." George is a very big man by any standard & he carries himself with the exuberance of a very big man. Back in '65, he probably weighed a solid 230; his style of dress is hard to describe for no extant term quite gets it. I'll call it post-Hemingway baroque. For daytime wear it could include anything from a foundry-worker's coveralls to a purple tuxedo. His hair was just going gray & was so thick, long, & wild, it looked as though it had never faced the shears of a trained barber. I thought immediately of Theodore Roethke during his greenhouse years.

Though both were superb readers, their styles had almost nothing in common. Coulette read from his wonderful first book, *The War of the Secret Agents,* with an almost icy precision which beautifully suited the work. Essentially a shy man, he spoke little between poems, which was a shame for he possessed a fine sense of irony. Fortunately it came through in the poems. Then it was George's turn. First he thanked Henri for the reading & for his companionship during their tour, & then he turned to his poems & opened up his enormous voice & let go. Nothing was more obvious than that he liked performing; he put his whole self into it. First his poems, serious & visionary, driven forward by the fury of his energy, original, surreal, & unpredictable:

> I celebrate the swans with their invisible
> plumage of steam, I pursue fragrant bullets
> in the blue meadows, I observe in the reeds
> the sacraments of cellulose, I seek
> my lost ancestors.
>
> *(from "How My Life Is Spent")*

He followed them with a short collection of riotously funny found poems: Yes, this was truly the editor of what was becoming the most original & readable American poetry magazine in decades. I had asked myself before what was it that gave *kayak* such a potent & unified vision of the America of the Sixties in spite of the fact it seemed to have room for almost every talented poet not writing Petrarchan sonnets (although George had published a wonderful parody of one), many poets who couldn't even speak to each other: the answer was here in the character of George Hitchcock. Before the reading ended, George did something I have never seen another poet do: he turned to the audience & asked if there were anyone among us who would like to come forward & join the reading. No one took him up on it, so he turned to me & said, "Come on, Phil, you must have something to read." I was so startled I declined the invitation. Generosity of this nature is not something one encounters very often on the reading trail, which is, unfortunately, where one is apt to see poets at their very worst, full of self & empty of a sense of others. George, I realized, was entirely sincere, & a word came into my mind that I have rarely brought to bear on anyone, much less a touring poet: Bountiful. This guy had a lot to give & the energy & character not to tire of giving it.

Everything I've learned about George that first day I never unlearned, for he is exactly who he is: an adult in total possession of himself. There is no pose, no effort to charm—indeed he is naturally likeable & charming—and his personality is so rich that every time I've been with him for a day or more, I've been rewarded by new discoveries. The man who founded & edited for over a decade a truly great poetry journal had to be tough at times, had to posses high standards & his own vision of the poetry that mattered. As a non-academic he had no experience with committee decisions regarding artistic merit. George is a strong man with strong beliefs, one who is able to live with the dislike of others. (Have a look at his testimony before HUAC, & you'll get an idea of what he thinks of committee decision & of courting dislike when it's worth treasuring.) You could say of George that what you see is what you get, but it wouldn't be true: you get more than you ever see.

Some years later George asked me if I'd like to do a book with Kayak Press. By this time he'd done books by Charles Simic & Raymond Carver, so the press—though a small one—was on the map of poetry. He warned me that it would be illustrated & that I would have no say in the matter as well as no say in the choice of the cover or in any aspect of the design. He wouldn't fool with the poems & I wouldn't fool with the production of the book, which was fine. I was by this time a devoted reader of the magazine as well as a delighted contributor, so I had a clear notion of just how eccentric his sense of illustration could be. I'd been having a terrible time finding a publisher for my third poetry collection. It had wandered from editor to editor collecting rejections. George had already printed the poem "They Feed They Lion" in *kayak*, but the manuscript of that title was sleeping in the editorial offices of Wesleyan University Press where it would be awakened to a second rejection, but I had another collection, which I gave George. The submission & acceptance took place through the mail & required no contract or paperwork. I received a copy of the new book, *Red Dust*, a month ahead of schedule. It looked like no book I'd ever seen before, & I liked it. I even liked the poems; I hadn't had time to tire of them. In the letter that came with that first copy was a check which amounted to my royalties: he didn't want the trouble of screwing around with the bookkeeping; he was sure he'd sell all the copies, so here it was in dollars. That too never happened before or again. It may be a first in the history of poetry.

For many years I did not take George's poetry as seriously as it merited. I think I may have been so enraptured by his presence that I assumed that was the entrée of the feast he is. In 1984 he sent me a copy of a large collection, *The Wounded Alphabet*, which contains several extraordinary poems in his distinctive voice, poems as extraordinary as anything being written. Here is one, "End of Ambition," though I could have chosen "There's No Use Asking" or "His Last Words":

END OF AMBITION

when I get there the last
mail has been sorted
my friends gather
in their arctic parkas
they speak a language
I don't understand
they've put off their
togas I don't recognize
the pumping station
or the grimy collier
docked at the pier

I'd waited a long time
I sat in the tower
for months weaving
these wings out of rage
& envy I'd almost
forgotten the song
of the parapets &
the green vision
we saw from the cliffs

perhaps it's too late
perhaps they no longer
care the tide is out
the rules of flight
have been altered &
maybe there's no way now

to get beyond the clouds
of white corpuscles
& the tongues
darting & skimming
over the parched
mud-flats

To understate the matter, George gave the American poetry world three price-less gifts, his own writing, *kayak*—the finest poetry magazine of my era—, and his complex & unusual presence which served as a model for so many of us: the model of the poet as a total human being (as my mother would have said, a *men-sch*). I've heard poets not a fraction as dedicated & gifted as George whine about how much they'd given America & how little it had given back. I've heard oth-ers literally cry for the lack of fame & fortune they'd suffered because they chose to be poets. I can't imagine anyone who'd been mentored by George, officially or otherwise, crying over his or her lack of celebrity. He or she would be much more likely to greet the closed door to fame with suitable defiance & if words were required they'd likely be "Live free or die!" George is one of those Americans who spring up all too rarely, those originals who make you proud of your birthright: he loves this country so much he's spent his life trying to make it a place worthy of its stated principles, its land & its people. Like anyone strug-gling to make his or her America a decent society, George has known a history of losses; meeting him you would never know it. His years in the labor move-ment have taught him all a person needs to know about loyalty, independence & human dignity. His years as a gardener & an actor taught him the value of beauty & new growth. Those of us who shared his years as an editor & writer learned by example that a person can give his energy & heart to worthy ventures even in a corrupt society & never compromise. For those of us to whom he has been both mentor & friend—a huge portion of my generation of American poets—the gifts have been enormous & no doubt different for each of us. I believe we all learned that the age-old conflict between art & life was nonsense: in George's case nothing was more obvious than art was his life & his life was an art. His laughter—like a totem against depression & defeat—I carry with me always and his lesson that hard work in the service of good cause is like poetry, its own reward. ✒

THE UNSAYABLE, THE UNKNOWABLE, AND YOU

by David St. John

What is the place of mystery in poetry? How is mystery different from obscurity? Can there be a poetry of desire that neglects mystery? What constitutes beauty in poetry? Is it natural simplicity? Is it exquisite elaboration?

I believe poetry provides not "poems" — those decorative *objects* to be pressed like dead leaves between the pages of anthologies — but, instead, both delicate and complex acts of perception, models of consciousness which help illuminate our world. The function of style in poetry is to help mirror that rendered act of perception, of consciousness, that the poet wishes to enact for the reader. Poems are themselves dramas of consciousness (or, in this postmodern world, perhaps we must say *the consciousness of the self-consciousness of consciousness!*); some stand as lyric enactments of perception, some as reflective, meditative, or narrative enactments. A poem's style is its meaning, because that style is the true mirror, the exact mechanism, and the presentational enactment of the poem's process of perception.

Think of style as the lens through which the poem is projected, the lens through which the poem is quite literally read. Style, which makes explicit those characteristics particular to any given poet's act of perception, is the way by which we, as readers, *experience* a poem. A poem, as all poets know, is not a dead *thing*; it is vital and vibrant, and it is above all a sensual, intellectual, and visceral *experience*.

In the poems I admire most, I find that the poet's voice (that function of style) has been presenced almost holographically; that is, a three-dimensional speaking self has been enacted from a two-dimensional ink-and-paper stage. Unlike ourselves, poems and poetic voices do not have bodies, physical gestures, or tonal vocal colorations. The poem itself, *its* voice, must create these fuller dimensions for us. Style carves the feature of the face (the mask) that speaks the voice. Its body, too.

I think of the poems I admire most as being dramatic lyric enactments of self. Each poem becomes the staged (voiced) drama of the self, of consciousness, of the process of perception which makes us, individually, who we are — and which distinguishes each of us as the poets we are or wish to be. We create these distinguishing differences and make them known to a reader through the stylistic choices and manifestations of the poem. In the work, at least, we are who we write.

This act of self-creation is an essential, underlying element of our poetry. (Though clearly some poets consider this an irresistible temptation to engage in a little self-mythologizing as well.) Think of it this way — just as we take on a poetic mask in a dramatic monologue, a mask we shape quite carefully in the course of such a monologue, developing specific features and emotional concerns for our persona, we are likewise forging an individual mask in every poem in which we say "I." How close to "ourselves" or our "true selves" we wish this individual poetic mask to be is a question of aesthetic choice and temperament. Even when we say "I" in a poem it is the written mask, the inscribed mask of "I" who speaks. For many poets the ambition of their poetry is to forge a mask that resembles them as closely as possible; they wish to create (enact) a poetic speaking voice which they feel most closely approximates their "own" voice. Even those who feel that the more style*less* the voice, the more "genuine" or authentic the speaking voice have to understand that this is in itself a stylistic choice and artistic decision. The mask of masklessness.

My point is very simple. A speaker in the Romantic tradition is figured in a poem by the same act of stylistic choice as any self-conscious, postmodern, highly gestural and self-referential speaker. It seems to me that neither choice necessarily lessens the poetic power, the majesty, of a speaking voice. I happen to find both Galway Kinnell and John Ashbery to be extraordinarily powerful and moving poetic voices and presences. However unlike their voices and aesthetic principles, they are both captivating and compelling poets. How one chooses to articulate the speaking self, and how one chooses to enact one's poetic presence in a poem, become a matter of artistic temperament, personal poetic values, and individual poetic ambition (I mean for the work, not for the career).

Let's return now to my opening questions concerning mystery and poetic beauty by recalling this marvelous quote from Mallarmé: "Everything holy that wishes to remain holy surrounds itself with mystery." And, lastly, let me offer this wisdom of Valéry: "The definition of beauty is easy; it is what drives us to desperation." 🖉

Acknowlegments

DAVID ALPAUGH: "What My Father Loved About Melmac" from the on-line journal *Caffeine Destiny*, © by David Alpaugh and used by permission of the author.

HOPE ALVARADO: "Introduction to a Portable Dorothy Parker" and "SJC" © by Hope Alvarado and used by permission of the author.

JOY ARBOR: "Sometimes In The Car" from *Santa Barbara Review*, Spring 1997, © 1997 by Joy Arbor and used by permission of the author.

CARLYE ARCHIBEQUE: "Things to say at a party when you don't want to be there" from *Beyond the Valley of the Contemporary Poets*, © 2001 by Carlye Archibeque and used by permission of the author.

CHARLES ARDINGER: "Island Music" © by Charles Ardinger and used by permission of the author.

SYLVIA BAR: "The Grail" © by Sylvia Bar and used by permission of the author.

DOROTHY BARRESI: "Love Koan" © by Dorothy Barresi and used by permission of the author.

TERRY BAT-SONJA: "I Wash You" © by Terry Bat-Sonja and used by permission of the author.

RICHARD BEBAN: "Summer Rain Sonnet For The Average Housefly" © by Richard Beban and used by permission of the author.

MARJORIE BECKER: "His Jesus Feet" © by Marjorie Becker and used by permission of the author.

MICHELLE BEN-HUR: "Tell Me Everything You Know About Mirrors" © by Michelle Ben-Hur and used by permission of the author.

AYANNA BENNETT: "The Shop" © by Ayanna Bennett and used by permission of the author.

DINAH BERLAND: "Water" © by Dinah Berland and used by permission of the author.

MEL BERNSTEIN: "Ragman" and "Seven Monkeys" © by Mel Bernstein and used by permission of the author.

WENDY BISHOP: "Grass: A Museum" from *Brahma 1978: 19-20* © by Wendy Bishop and used by permission of the author.

LAUREL ANN BOGEN: "Mystery Spot with Gaze Turned Inward" from *Washing a Language*, Red Hen Press, Fall 2002, © 2002 by Laurel Ann Bogen and used be permission of the author.

DEBORAH EDLER BROWN: "Faultlines" © by Deborah Edler Brown and used by permission of the author.

DERRICK BROWN: "Pussycat Interstellar Naked Hotrod Mofo Ladybug Lustblaster!" from *If Lovin' You is Wrong Then I don't Want to be Wrong*, Mood Organ Distributors, © 2001 by Derrick Brown and used be permission of the author.

MARK C. BRUCE: "The Pompeiian Couple" from *Rattle* Issue #13, Vo.6 #1, © Mark C. Bruce and used by permission of the author.

CHRISTOPHER BUCKLEY: "March 21st, & Spring Begins On Benito Juarez's Birthday in Mexico" from *Star Apocrypha*, Northwestern University Press, © 2001 by Christopher Buckley and used by permission of the author.

JOY BUCKLEY: "Panties In The Trash" © by Joy Buckley and used by permission of the author.

SUSAN BUIS: "8 Little Stories About Hands" © by Susan Buis and used by permission of the author.

STEPHEN BURDETTE: "Verlaine To Rimbaud" © by Stephen Burdette and used by permission of the author.

MARY CAHILL: "Vacation, One July" © by Mary Cahill and used by permission of the author.

DON "KINGFISHER" CAMPBELL: "Story of San Diego" © by Don "Kingfisher" Campbell and used by permission of the author.

JOHN D CASEY: "Anniversary" and "Minkowski" © by John D Casey and used by permission of the author.

MARY-MARCIA CASOLY: "Proof on the Verge, 1905" from *Transformations*, poetry by participants writing in workshops at the Oakland Museum of